HAM AND PETEI

AT 2000

General Editor: Leonard Chave

Historical adviser: Evelyn Pritchard

Illustrations by John Plant

RICHMOND LOCAL HISTORY SOCIETY

FOR THE HAM AMENITIES GROUP

2000

The original printing of this book
was made with assistance from
an 'Awards for All' grant

Historical introduction
© Evelyn Pritchard 2000
Illustrations © John Plant 2000
Main text © Ham Amenities
Group 2000

First published by the Ham Amenities
Group in May 2000
Published by the Richmond Local
History Society October 2000

ISBN 0 9522099 4 2

Typeset on an iMac in 11pt
Garamond and 10pt Arial MT
Condensed Light by
the General Editor

Printed and bound in Great Britain
by Redwood Books
Trowbridge
Wilts BA14 8RN

Contents

Foreword
by Lady Annabel Goldsmith

I was delighted when I heard that Ham Amenities Group were producing a book on Ham and Petersham at 2000, and I was both pleased and flattered to have been asked to write the foreword.

Ham is such a beautiful place that it is about time that someone gave it a write-up, extolling its virtues and great historical interest. Indeed the ability to be part of village life and yet be so close to London must be almost unique.

In January 1977 I took the momentous step of moving my family out of London to Ormeley Lodge by Ham Common. I did it with a certain amount of trepidation because although I personally had been brought up in the country, I had been living and bringing up my children for the past 22 years in London.

With a heavy heart I moved my five children, ages ranging from 2 years to 21, out of my enchanting cottage in South Kensington into Ormeley Lodge. By the following day all my doubts had vanished and I was as convinced as I am today that it was the best move of my life and I cannot imagine living anywhere else. Ham has all the advantages of the country with the added easy access to London, which, although the children initially went to excellent local schools, presented no problem when Jemima later went to school in London.

Going to sleep and waking to the sound of birds singing and the sight of trees and grass still remains a pleasure. Nowadays I simply cannot sleep in London because the sound of traffic has become alien to me.

Ham and Petersham, apart from their historical interest, are both beautiful and unspoilt. Ham Common, surrounded by period houses with its duck pond, occasional cricket matches and yearly Fair still manages to delight me after all these years. Then there is Richmond Park, King Charles I's original hunting park, 2,357 acres to roam in amongst the deer and with squirrels leaping from branch to branch and the occasional sight of a fox. Walking through the Park on one of those cold and frosty mornings, it is easy to imagine oneself anywhere in the English countryside.

I consider myself privileged to live in such a beautiful part of England and hope that I will do so for a long time to come.

Introduction

As with many other voluntary and charitable organisations, the question came up in 1999 as to how the Ham Amenities Group should celebrate the (so-called) Millennium. The first thought was of mounting a special exhibition at their Ham Fair (see pp.77–8) to trace some of the history of Ham; a small sub-committee under my chairmanship was formed to see this project through. Before the first meeting, however, I put forward an alternative idea: why not prepare a book telling what life is like in Ham at the present time? This was accepted, and I became General Editor, with Evelyn Pritchard co-opted as historical adviser.

An application for a Millennium Festival 'Awards for All' grant was successful, and an edition of 1000 copies was produced, the bulk of which was distributed free of charge to members of the Ham Amenities Group and the Ham and Petersham Association. Remaining copies were supplied in return for individual donations to four nominated charities, raising well over £600 in the process.

The book proved extremely popular with local people, but by the terms of our grant we were not able to make any profit from it, which precluded supplying copies to bookshops. We welcomed, therefore, the interest of the Richmond Local History Society, who were prepared to publish formally on our behalf when the subsidised edition was exhausted. Such publication is well within the spirit of the original grant, as they are themselves a Registered Charity. The first printing was only made possible by the voluntary help of some 100 contributors to the book; proceeds of the second printing will defray the costs of manufacture, but produce no great surplus for its publisher. We are very grateful that our local History Society are making this book more widely available, and ensuring that it will be kept in print for future generations of historians and for local residents. A few typographical corrections have been made, and a handful of errors of fact put right; otherwise this edition is identical with the original.

LEONARD CHAVE
(Vice-Chairman, Ham Amenities Group)

Editorial note

This book began as a project for recording the facilities and services enjoyed by the Ward of Ham and Petersham at the beginning of AD 2000. In discussion with those who were to compile the bulk of the information, it was realised that such an approach would be meaningless unless the historical background of the area and its facilities was also covered. Evelyn Pritchard, whose *Ham House and its owners through four centuries* and *A portrait of Ham in Early Victorian Times* have both become local classics, has acted as historical adviser, and has contributed a substantial opening chapter to the book. This chapter is not a history of England, or even of Ham and Petersham, but a depiction of the background against which the area, particularly Ham (where the social changes were more marked), grew and developed, and an account of the events that had a particular effect on the two villages. The Civil War is not mentioned, and the Second World War hardly at all, because neither were the cause of major social or material changes.

By showing how our area developed over the centuries and what caused these changes, it is hoped that the description of Ham and Petersham today, by several hands, will become more interesting. Cross-references have been made from later sections to the historical introduction; events and locations that have been written about already, and where information is easily obtainable have not been described in detail, but those who wish to understand any aspect in greater depth are referred to a Bibliography at the end of the text. A list of all articles relevant to Ham and Petersham in *Richmond History* can be found on pp.118–19; references to these are prefaced by H (e.g. [H10]), whilst those to the main Bibliography contain a numeral only (e.g. [15]). Most of the volumes of *Richmond History* are now out of print but can be found, in company with much other vital information, in the Richmond Local Studies Room at the Old Town Hall,

The Historical Background
by Evelyn Pritchard

WHAT'S IN A NAME?

Derived from the Old English word *Hamme*, meaning 'the place in the bend of a river', a quick glance at a map shows what a complete description of Ham the name gives. There is another Old English word *Ham*, meaning 'The home of' or a village. There could be a problem with a compound word, e.g. Twickenham, Amersham etc., in deciding which of the two Old English place name elements these names derive from. Fortunately, the single syllable Ham always derives from the former [1].

The origin of 'Petersham' is much more complicated. In AD 666 the Benedictine Abbey of St Peter, Chertsey, endowed certain lands, one of which was Piterichesham. This was spelt in various ways, including Patrices-ham, but because of the connection with Chertsey Abbey the name was taken to mean the home or enclosure of Peter. The hamlet, however, was already known by the name of Piterichesham well before the connection with Chertsey Abbey; place name experts are all agreed that the name comes from Patricius, meaning the home of Patrick, not Peter.

WHERE WAS THE FIRST LOCAL SETTLEMENT?

After the last Ice Age, in about 12,000 BC (the Mesolithic or Middle Stone Age), as the temperature began to rise, forests clothed the land; the sea rose, cutting off the British Isles from the Continent in around 7,500 BC. People began to come up and down the rivers in dugout canoes, still migrant hunter-gatherers. The whole of Ham Fields was a flood plain gravel terrace, the River Thames shallower and wider, particularly around the place that is now Ham. Because of the shallows, boats may well have had to be porteraged, i.e. hauled up on shore and carried overland, making Ham an ideal stopover place to rest, mend boats or even make new ones.

In the New Stone Age or Neolithic period, approximately 4,500 BC, people arrived who were intermediate between hunter-gatherers and farmers, knowing how to grow wheat and keep cattle, sheep and pigs. These people were looking for places to settle; Ham would appear to be an ideal place with the shallows giving easy access to gravel banks, while the river would cater for most of their food needs, with shellfish, waterfowl, fish — with salmon an important item — and probably beaver. Apart from the well-drained gravel of the site, within a mile or two a number of soil types — sand, alluvium, brick earth and heavily forested London Clay — would have provided a range of habitats for mammals and birds that could be hunted. Along and astride a gravel bank, parallel to the river that may have provided shelter, a large surface collection of archaeological materials was found. This was south of a place named Coldharbour in later history, part of Ham Manor Farm in the eighteenth century, not far from the Young Mariners' Base in the twentieth century (National Grid Ref. TQ 164 724). These artifacts are known as the Edwards Collection [2]. The archaeological finds consisted of tools, including a range of sizes of axes and adzes, scrapers, awls, chisels and knives; there were also arrowheads, hammerstones, cores, flakes and other waste. These tools were of top quality Downs flint, most probably carried from the North Downs, whereas other flint sites in the area were of poor quality river gravel: the quantity of waste material suggests that flint knapping was done on site. The number of small axes present suggested that tree felling was not their primary purpose, but that in conjunction with the adzes it represented a considerable amount of woodworking. Ground axes indicate a permanent rather than a nomadic existence.

In conjunction with material from the site in other collections there is evidence of almost continuous occupation from early pre-history to the present. These artifacts are as follows:

large fragments of Bronze Age and of late Iron Age or early Romano/ British pots and urns.

pieces of quernstone — used for grinding corn.

gun flints, Old English.

coins: worn Charles II farthing 1672/79; worn, broken William III farthing 1698/99.

clay pipes, early seventeenth–mid eighteenth century.

wig curlers, eighteenth century.

Coldharbour, the name by which the site was known, was not recorded until the fourteenth century as Coldherbeghe or Coldharburgh (Middle English), meaning a cold shelter. The name occurred in many areas of England, usually attached to farms or homesteads.

An important requirement for a settlement site was water. There were two small settlements at Latchmere and Sudbrook, where there was water and meadowland from streams. The Latchmere stream (Latchmere = Sluggish Brook) flowed along below the ridge of what is now Richmond Park, changing its name to the Sudbrook or South Brook where it entered the Park in the area of Ham Gate. In early times there was a settlement of ten houses at Sudbrook (see p.6), that had reduced to only one house by the seventeenth century. The streams are now mainly underground in pipes.

From the first Neolithic settlement, over the centuries the woodland was very gradually cleared, each generation adding to site by cutting down wild growth and woodland round the edges, so fanning out over the surrounding area to produce land for a small farming community. The animals grazing on cleared land would prevent the regrowth of saplings. From this time, Ham was an agricultural community, remaining so until almost the end of the nineteenth century.

Nothing has been recorded in Petersham of Neolithic or other ancient remains. After the Coldharbour settlement began (see p.3), it seems reasonable to expect that the people would have fanned out to hunt and to begin to clear land for rudimentary farming, particularly away from the marshy ground near the river, on higher, drier ground. Sudbrook, Latchmere and Petersham were likely to have been colonised in this way, for the Sudbrook ran through the hamlet as an open ditch to River Lane before emptying into the river.

A.D. AGRICULTURE AND THE OPEN FIELDS

Moving now from BC to AD no evidence has been found of a Roman settlement in Ham. By 450 the Anglo-Saxon invasions began, spreading over Britain and lasting until the coming of the Normans in 1066.

Patricesham (see p.2) occurs in the Domesday book of 1086. The Survey says 'There is a church', i.e. St Peter's (see p.16); also two fisheries (weirs), one of 1,000 eels, the other of 1,000 lampreys. The hamlet was not referred to as Petersham until 1550.

During this period much of England became a land of villages and hamlets farmed by the Open or Common Field system. The nucleus of Ham appears to have been in what is now Ham Street, from where the Common ends near the pond until just past the Sandy Lane turning, when it became a track that was later called Ham Lane, running more or less straight to the river.

There would have been two very large fields, one stretching from Ham Street down to the river, the second right up to part of what is now Richmond Park and across it to Kingston Hill. The fields were divided into strips, a parcel of strips all running in the same direction made up a Furlong or Shott, each Furlong being given a name. Each owner — probably those who had cleared the land of trees — had scattered holdings of strips, not contiguous with one another. This arrangement made a fair division of land, some good and some poor; the meadow land lying near the river was also divided amongst various persons, while the rest of the land was waste or common where animals grazed. Each generation cleared more land around the edges of the settlement until the fullest extent was reached. A windmill for grinding corn had been provided by 1292, also a weir (fishery), in the Thames.

Farming by the Open Field method distributed the land fairly, but limited what an individual could do with his land, for the same crop would have to be grown in each strip in a Furlong or Shott and harvested at the same time [3]. Enclosures of land on a small scale began in the fourteenth century by two owners agreeing to exchange or buy strips from one another, to make a compact holding of a small field that could be hedged or separated off as an enclosure. This went on intermittently and at a varying pace in every century, speeding up about 1830 and especially by Parliamentary Acts and Awards between 1750 and 1850. Ham apparently had no Enclosure Acts or Awards applied to it and was unusual in having areas of Open Fields still there for most of the nineteenth century.

While Ham remained as an agricultural area, Petersham gives the impression of having grown as an overflow from Richmond, which had a Royal Palace for centuries, attracting courtiers and others trying for a place at the Court, or the ear of the King, together with hundreds of servants. Richmond would have expanded in all directions, including towards Petersham. A small place of only 600 acres, it seems to have attracted mainly aristocrats who built large houses, together with their servants and gardeners.

PARISH BOUNDARIES

When parish boundaries were drawn in Medieval times, this was done in such a way that each had a section of the woods and heath on the high ground of the Richmond Park site, wherever possible the land in between being cultivated in the form of open fields or enclosures. Two boundary stones of 1843 that look like truncated bollards are still in position, one on the Petersham Road opposite 'The Poplars' (see map on p.30), the other on the raised footpath of the Lower Ham Road (in Kingston), near the 'Albany' flats [8]. Parish boundaries remained the same for centuries. In fact, it was only after about 1860 when the Government began to interfere in local affairs that parish boundaries began to change.

The boundary of Petersham with Richmond has always been recorded as in the vicinity of Nightingale Lane, the steep, narrow lane from the top of Richmond Terrace down to the main Richmond/Kingston Road. Thus Petersham, roughly one third the size of Ham, included part of the Star and

Garter Hill with any houses on the top of it, together with Sudbrook.

SUDBROOK

Sudbrook was an ancient settlement mentioned in a charter of Henry II in 1266, which was a distinct hamlet of Petersham. It was an ideal place for a settlement, watered by the Latchmere Brook which changed its name to the South Brook or Sudbrook as it passed through to what is now Richmond Park near Ham Gate, eventually emptying into the River Thames at the bottom of River Lane in Petersham, providing fresh water and meadowland for the grazing of animals. Early tax records list John Reyner of Southbrook, Roger de Southbrook and Alice his wife, Geoffrey de Southbrook, Walter, William and John Watte of Southbrook and so on, adding up to about ten houses. But in the reign of Edward III there were entries under the community of Petersham, suggesting that the people from Sudbrook were moving into Petersham village. By the 1700s only one house in Sudbrook survived; Hatch Court, owned by John Burchett, with seventeen acres of land, with stables, orchard, garden and outbuildings. In 1715 John Burchett surrendered all his holdings to John, 2nd Duke of Argyll, with his land in Sudbrook augmented by 30 acres leased to him by George I; the hero of the Marlborough Wars, 'Red John of the Battles', grandson of Elizabeth, Countess of Dysart, had a new house built by Gibbs between 1715–19. Sudbrook House is now the Club House of Richmond Golf Club (see p.73).

THE ENCLOSURE OF RICHMOND PARK

The year 1637 brought a great change to Ham and Petersham. King Charles I 'was excessively affected to hunting and the sports of the field'. He wanted to make a great park for red and fallow deer between Richmond and Hampton Court, where he owned wastes and woodland, but unfortunately some parishes had common in those wastes and many gentlemen and farmers had good farms intermingled with the wastes, either by inheritance or copyhold for lives or years. Charles was willing to pay over the odds for the land but was determined to have it. Many gave way quickly, others were more obstinate. Eventually he began to build a wall before people had consented to part with their land or commons. Worried that by degrees they would be shut out of both, they gave in and sold.

The parishes affected were Kingston, Wimbledon, Putney, Mortlake, Richmond, Petersham and Ham. Although Charles I's Park is called Richmond Park, Ham was the greatest loser of land, Richmond the least. Of the roughly 2,357 acres enclosed, Ham lost 895 acres, Petersham 306, Richmond only 69. About 400 acres of the land lost to Ham was common land [4, 5].

As has already been mentioned (p.4), Ham stretched across the site of the park to a strip along Kingston Hill, the enclosure effectively cutting that strip off from the rest of the village. The farmers would have lost their fields and rents, the Manor lost about half its Tithes. Further, the inhabitants would have lost their right of collecting firewood from half the Common and of grazing their animals there.

Charles I executed a Deed between himself and the freeholders and copyholders of inheritance and tenants for lives or years of Ham and Petersham, stating that they have willingly agreed to his taking 265 acres of Petersham and 483 acres of Ham into his new Park for which he has paid £4,000 to be divided between them, in proportion to their holdings. In return, they have agreed to renounce all their rights in this common land. Further, the remaining waste or common land not taken into the new Park will be for the sole benefit and profit of the tenants, neither the King, his heirs nor successors or any of the Farmers of the Manors shall henceforth take any benefit or profit from them. Apart from some minor nibblings around the edges, the Common occupies the same area today as it did when this Deed was proclaimed in 1637.

In 1751 there were rumblings of discontent about what was happening in Richmond Park. It was reported that in the first instance great care had been taken to make it plain that gates were to be placed in relevant positions so that communication between neighbouring towns was not hindered. This had been done; certainly by 1751 two rights of way were kept open and the poor were allowed in to gather firewood. But Princess Amelia, daughter of George II, had been made Ranger of the Park, and she was trying to exclude the people. John Lewis, a brewer of Richmond, challenged her by bringing an action against Martha Gray, the gatekeeper who refused him admittance. The trial at Kingston Assizes on 3 April 1758 was won by Lewis, who was given the choice of ladderstiles or doors at the gates, electing for the former. In 1758 these were fixed at Ham Gate. Lewis complained again that the ladderstile steps were so far apart that children and old men were unable to climb up. The Justice ruled that they must be constructed so that old women also may be able to get up. In 1761 Princess Amelia gave up her Rangership and left the Park.

THE BEGINNINGS OF THE GROWTH OF HAM

Ham House was built in 1610 by Sir Thomas Vavasour, Knight Marshal to

James I. He was responsible for the discipline of the Court, wherever it happened to be — Whitehall, St James's, Richmond, Hampton Court or Windsor. From his house, he could get readily to all these places in his barge by river. Most of the other large houses in Ham and Petersham appeared in the eighteenth century, particularly in the second half, many being re-buildings of older and smaller houses on the same sites [H16, H17].

While Petersham took the overflow of aristocrats from Richmond, where there had been a Royal palace and courtiers clustered, Ham only aspired in the main to gentry, senior army, navy and retired East India Company personnel, plus others styled as 'independents' — annuitants, those with money in Government Funds and property. As the eighteenth century progressed, merchants began to build or buy property in Ham, to bring their families out from the smells, noise and plagues of London.

In 1800, Ham was still an agricultural community, the greatest number of inhabitants being agricultural labourers. There were three large farms, all owned by Lord Dysart of Ham House, worked by tenant farmers, two side-by-side in Ham Street, one across the other side of the Richmond/Kingston road. They were mixed farms, the main crops were wheat, barley and oats, with orchards for fruit; cattle, sheep and pigs, geese and chickens. It was still subsistence agriculture, with the aim of feeding the local population. Most of the larger houses kept a cow, a pig or sow and chickens, a kitchen garden for vegetables and some fruit trees. The maltster was the tenant of one of the Ham Street farms, with his malt house across what later became the junction of Lock Road and Ham Street.

The village was virtually self-sufficient, with blacksmiths, wheelwright, carpenters, bricklayers, painters, boot and shoe makers and repairers, with dressmakers, needlewomen and tailors for those who could not make their own clothes. A few shops were scattered throughout the village, mainly butchers, bakers and grocers.

It must be stressed that Ham was a very small village — in 1800 the population was only 500, probably in 80 houses at the most. More cottages were built in Ham Street around 1820, and 31 more houses along the Petersham Road from the New Inn in the late 1830s. By 1851 the population had risen to 1,324, the number of houses to 236. Lighting was by rushlights or candles, water from wells and pumps; there was little or no sanitation. Most cottages had one room on the ground floor, two upstairs, no kitchen, bathroom or inside lavatory. Heating was by open fires on which all the cooking was done. Some had a wash house or shed outside to act as a scullery or laundry [8].

There were virtually no roads in Ham; the only ones there were made of stones and gravel, dusty in summer and quagmires in winter. The only roads were the Richmond/Kingston road, Ham Street, Sandy Lane (all gravelled), while Back Lane ran behind Ham Street, parallel to it, as a way for men, carts and animals to get from the farms to the fields. Any cottages built along this lane were called 'in the fields'.

In 1817, Benjamin Barnard, a banker, made a footpath from the main road to his house next to the Ham Gate to Richmond Park; this was called Barnard's Footpath, and is now Ham Gate Avenue.

Church Road was built around 1832 from the new church of St Andrew's on the Common to the main road, later extended to Latchmere House, later still to the gate to Richmond Park.

During this period a school was started in 1817, and a Union Workhouse was built in Kingston in response to the Poor Law Amendment Act of 1834, to which Ham was supposed to send its paupers [8]. These will be dealt with separately under the appropriate headings (pp.18–19, 11).

THE GROWTH OF PETERSHAM

Petersham had only one large common field, one farm, a Common on the steep side of Star and Garter Hill and meadows down by the river. There seems to have been no defined centre to the village; when there was a maypole it appears to have been erected in the area which is now at the top of the avenue to Ham House and the German School. Houses were mainly along the Petersham Road, a few down Sudbrook Lane, River Lane and Hazel Lane, while Sandy Lane had no houses until the twentieth century.

The Petersham Hearth Tax of 1664 lists only 25 houses, of which eight had either one or no hearths, so paid no tax; 44% had from 4 to 9 hearths, quite substantial houses; a Lady Bellamount had 11 hearths, Ham House had 24 and Colonel Panton's was down as 'not known'. He had rebuilt Old Petersham Lodge in the Park, and also built Petersham House on the main road near the Church, both substantial houses, but the tax men may not have been sure which to charge him for, if he was not in residence.

Except in its early years, Petersham could not be classed as an agricultural community. In 1852, when the Tithe Map was drawn, 250 of its 600 acres had been enclosed in Richmond Park, while 123 acres (33% of the total available) were lawns, pleasure grounds and sites of houses. In 1841 there were 37 agricultural labourers, 36 gardeners and 180 servants; by 1851 the number of agricultural labourers had dropped to 12.

The population of Ham rose from 557 to 1,933 by 1891, while the population of Petersham only rose from 422 to 566 in the same period. When Ham was converting to a market garden economy and building new roads in the 1890s, Petersham was growing only 12 acres of wheat and very little else except for 24 acres of greens. In 1895, greens were the only vegetable being grown, but orchards and nursery gardens had increased from 18 to 95 acres. Cattle had been drastically reduced, but surprisingly the number of sheep had risen to 100. Petersham seemed content to slumber on; fortunately no new roads were built until the 1920s.

LOCAL GOVERNMENT

Ham village was administered mainly by a parochial Vestry, in effect a petty parliament of the inhabitants through a set of parish officers. The Vestry was so called because its nominal meeting place was the Vestry room of the Church, but as there was no church in Ham until 1832 [6], they met instead at the New Inn on Ham Common. They were expected, with the assistance of the officers, to carry out almost the whole of local government in subordination to the magistrates, or Justices of the Peace. Between them, the parish officers were responsible for the relief of the poor, maintenance of the highways, drainage and sanitation, the Church and its affairs, encroachments on the Common, regulation of animals on the Common, maintenance of law and order, setting and collecting various taxes and making by-laws if necessary. The management of Ham was fairly evenly divided between gentry and professional men, the large farmers, tradesmen and craftsmen, plus one or two gardeners and publicans. For most Parish officers it was essential that they could read and write, a limitation on choice in an era when 50% of the population could not even sign their name [8].

As the population rose, it soon became clear that these responsibilities were becoming almost too much for a small village to cope with. It also became clear that the Government was aiming to remove power from the Vestries by enacting a series of Acts with the purpose of transferring it to more centralised control. An Act of 1858 gave authority for Local Boards to be set up to take over some responsibilities from the Vestry, each Board being concerned with one aspect, such as Highways, Health, etc., the number of members on a Local Board to be determined by the ratepayers and owners. But these Acts were permissive, not mandatory, so tended to be largely ignored in Ham. In 1871, however, an overall Local Government Board was formed to regulate and control all Local Boards; it had much wider powers than the individual Boards, removing the right of the parishioners in Vestry to approve the formation of a Board by vote, taking this decision to itself.

There was an earlier Act that had always been mandatory – the Poor Law Amendment Act of 1834. This transferred the responsibility for the poor from each parish to an elected Board of Guardians of a Union of parishes. They had to build and run a Union workhouse in a local town to which all the parishes were to send their poor. This was an attempt to make a more efficient system and reduce the burden of the Poor Rate.

The Board of Guardians was made up of 21 elected members from Kingston and all the surrounding parishes, Ham having usually one or two representatives. Theoretically, this should have put an end to outdoor relief, but Ham, as always, seemed determined to do its own thing. Outdoor relief continued, as did the office of Overseer until around 1880. The number of persons sent to the workhouse from Ham has not been found to be more than eight or nine, sometimes only six or none at all. Additionally, by 1848 there were eight almshouses in Ham for elderly poor, some for married, some for single people. On occasion two widows or two widowers would be put together. By 1892, three of the old almshouses had been demolished, and six new ones, for three married couples and three single persons, had been erected and endowed by the Hon. Mrs Tollemache of Ham House as a memorial to her husband, Algernon Gray Tollemache, MP, who had died on 6 June 1892. The endowment was sufficient to provide 7 shillings per week to each occupant.

In course of time, the Board of Guardians had also assumed responsibility for health matters, continuing to do so until the Public Health Act of 1872, when Rural Sanitary Authorities were constituted [8].

Petersham became joined to the Borough of Richmond in 1892. In 1894, under the provisions of the Local Government Act of that year, Ham became a civil parish, governed by an Urban District Council of ten elected members taking the place of the Local Boards.

TRANSPORT

It has already been mentioned (p.9) that the roads in Ham were extremely bad, quagmires in winter, so dusty in summer that they had to be watered. About the 1750s a Turnpike road [18], with Toll Houses, was constructed from London down Kingston Hill, then through Kingston Town to Portsmouth and Southampton, with a better surface making journeys along it much easier and quicker. Transport would have been by coach if it could be afforded, by horse if owned or hired, or by carrier's cart. Local roads, what there was of them, were still gravelled until well into the third quarter of the nineteenth century.

In 1846, the London and South Western Railway came to the newly-built Richmond station [H15, 19], running 17 trains a day to London; by 1864 these had increased to 24. At first the London trains finished at Nine Elms, then later the line was extended to Waterloo where passengers could change for the City. The carriages were 1st, 2nd and 3rd Class, with wooden seats in the latter, not much more comfort in 2nd. The complaints are familiar to us today — not enough trains, always late, with long waits for connections at junctions, crowded, too expensive and to the wrong places (women wanted to go to the West End). Until the late nineteenth century the majority of the population could not afford to travel by train, except when special ones were laid on for excursions to Richmond Park, Bushy Park, the Riverside or Wimbledon Common.

In the last quarter of the nineteenth century six companies provided trains to Richmond from central London, including in 1877 the District Line service to and from Mansion House. The railway was having an effect upon the population of Ham, by making it possible for more professional men to live there, commuting daily to their offices in the City. Flys, a kind of horse-drawn taxi, would ply for hire at Richmond station. It was thought at first that the trains would ring the knell for the carriers' carts, but in fact the reverse was the case. It was much cheaper for both people and parcels to go by this method and they were also needed to link into the rail network. Ham had one carrier in 1841, two in 1851 and five in 1861. Samuel Meredew ran a service from his house on the Petersham Road to London every Tuesday, Thursday and Saturday, as well as other local services. By 1899, Carter Paterson & Co. Ltd, The London Delivery Service Ltd, Pickford & Co. and J Little were all providing carrier services from Ham to London.

By 1845 horse-drawn omnibuses passed along the Richmond/Kingston road to and from London two or three times a day. It was not until 1905 that the New London and Suburban Co. introduced motor buses onto their Richmond to Surbiton route. Soon there was a service to Surbiton from Richmond station through Ham on the 65 route to Kingston, at 20 min. intervals between 9.30am and 9.10pm; the fare to the Dysart Arms was twopence and to Kingston Market fivepence.

It is not clear how Ham roads were lit, if at all, until about the 1840s, when there were five oil lamps, probably around Ham Green. In 1846 the Richmond Gas Co. was formed, soon running out pipes to supply Petersham. In 1852 the Ham Vestry eventually decided to have their original five lamps lit by gas — these were the only lights in the whole of the parish: they were of the bat-wing type worked by a pulley. Twenty years later, Ham was still only lit round the Green, where most of the large houses were, possibly with one lamp near the Royal Oak on the corner of Sandy Lane, but still none up Church Road to St Andrew's [8].

THE RIVER THAMES

This was a main traffic artery for centuries. In 1197, by a Charter of Richard I, the City of London exercised supervision over the whole navigable Thames [20, 21, 22]; in 1857 an Act gave the Thames Conservancy body control of the river from Staines to the estuary; on 21 December 1908, the part of the river from the Teddington/Twickenham boundary was transferred to the reconstituted Port of London Authority. There is a pillar marking this division on the Ham riverbank.

People like the Dysarts of Ham House had their own barge while others could be rowed by watermen in wherries — in 1770 it cost 4s to be rowed from London to Twickenham. while in 1828 London to Richmond was 1s 3d. All heavy loads were carried by barges, these having to be towed by teams of men or horses, walking along the bargeway or towing path. This was on the Middlesex bank from Isleworth to Twickenham Ait, then returned to the Surrey bank, where horses towed from River Lane to One Tree, an old elm that had been a landmark for mariners for centuries. 70 barge horses were stabled near the Fox and Duck (see p.20) and led down River Lane as required.

The stretch of towpath was owned by Lord Dysart, who had erected a Toll Bar at each end of his land, charging 3d per horse — a heavy load could require twelve horses to tow it. Despite these charges and navigation taxes from the City of London it was still four times cheaper to move goods by water than on land.

The first half of the nineteenth century saw the peak of barge traffic on English rivers and canals. In 1849, in one week 20 tons of goods were carried from London to Ham in one barge, 9 barges with a total of 219 tons to Twickenham and one with 20 tons to Petersham. Many loads went up to London from Kingston and Ham with barley for the breweries, coming back with coal, which is why men described themselves as maltster and coal merchant, two very different trades. Well into the second half of the nineteenth century there were 100 to 200 barges per week passing through.

TEDDINGTON LOCKS

These were first constructed in 1811, Lord Dysart providing land for a Lockkeeper's house on the Ham side, larger locks being built in 1854 and 1904, but the future of the river as a main carrier of goods was doomed, despite the fact that the first steamer passed through the lock in 1843. The culprit was the railway (see p.12), which soon began to draw business away from the river. Railway competition led to decreasing traffic and dwindling revenues, and gradually after about 1853, the river became a pleasure waterway rather than a commercial one. In 1867 the Thames Conservancy receipts from lock tolls were £2,550 from barges and £1,020 from pleasure craft, but in 1887, despite steam barges, tolls were down to £1,174 for commercial traffic and up to £3,805 from pleasure boats.

As early as 1843 a house of entertainment had been built on Eel Pie Island, where many came to dine on eel pies, for which it was famous. Later, people came up the river to Kingston. where Nuthalls in the Market Place was a famous rendezvous where rowing boats, skiffs and punts could tie up for tea. The banqueting suite was also THE place to go for any celebrations. The Nuthalls building, very decorative, still exists.

Permission was sought for a footbridge in 1882, to connect Ham to Teddington, which was opened in 1888.

FERRIES

Ham and Petersham on the Surrey bank of the river were isolated from Teddington and Twickenham on the Middlesex bank apart from the ferries, when the only bridges were London Bridge and the second to be built, the wooden one at Kingston. They grew in importance after Ham House was built. A ferry belonged to the Duchess of Lauderdale in the 1670s, the surviving lease being to Richard Blower. It ran from Ferry Lane in Twickenham, near the Old Swan Inn, to a point in Ferry field on the Surrey bank, just past the end of Eel Pie Island. This was a little further along towards Kingston than the present car park at the river end of Ham Street. It took passengers, animals and goods. The only other ferry nearby was the Richmond ferry from Twickenham to near the site of the present Richmond Bridge (built 1774–7), which took horses and coaches. There was frequent trouble with unlicensed ferrymen. By the Act of 1859, a ferryman was required to be a licensed waterman, but the Act exempted existing ferries.

In the early years of the nineteenth century, Ferry Cottage was built for the ferryman on the Twickenham side and a wooden building on the Surrey bank where his wife sold refreshments. In later years Mr Champion, the ferryman, kept three boats which took 30, 20 and 15 persons. The lease of the ferry was £30 per annum.

In 1901 Marble Hill House was purchased for public use and opened to the public two years later; in 1902 the towpath was made a public highway. The ferry was used by workmen making for buses and trams from Twickenham to London, and at the weekends for leisure traffic and the Sunday evening concerts on Eel Pie Island. In 1908 Walter Hammerton obtained a licence from the Port of London Authority to moor a fairly large floating boathouse by the towpath near Marble Hill. He had boats for hire, took passengers to the Surrey bank and in 1909 advertised a ferry service at 1*d* per head which ran to steps just past Ham House towards Richmond.

After some years of wrangling, Lord Dysart as owner and Will Champion as lessee brought an action against Hammerton, claiming the sole right of ferry services between Ham and Twickenham. The Judge ruled that Lord Dysart was entitled to a franchise ferry, but that Hammerton was dealing with new traffic and not infringing his rights, thus upholding the rights of the people using public riverside lands to be conveyed across the Thames at convenient points [23].

The 1920s were prosperous for the Thames at Ham, with the hire of skiffs and punts and the pleasure steamers running up and down the river. In 1948, Sir Lionel Tollemache gave Ham House to the National Trust and on 5 December 1949 Buckminster Estates, Trustees for the Dysart family, sold the old ferry rights and the ferry cottage. With the increase in ownership and usage of cars there was a gradual decrease in the popularity of the river so that it became virtually impossible to make a living, even at 2*d* per trip, and the old ferry closed in 1961. It was taken up again in 1964 for a short period, but eventually the franchise ferry closed for good.

THE POST

Until 1839 letters were folded and sealed with wax; there were no envelopes or adhesive stamps. Postage was assessed according to the distance it had to travel and the number of sheets of paper used, taking into account the weight for heavy letters or packages. At first letters had to be collected from the Receiving Office and paid for; later there were limited delivery services for a fee. As an example, a single sheet of paper less than one ounce in weight could travel up to 80 miles from London for threepence, while two or more sheets under one ounce would cost ninepence. Government officials and MPs could frank their letters for free delivery [17]. The Receiving Office at Ham was at Mr Payne's house on Ham Common, which was next to the National Orphans' Home (now South Lodge). The penny post was introduced in 1840, with adhesive stamps. Ham and Petersham's post was in the London collection area, letters arriving in Richmond, then by foot post from there at 8am, 1pm and 9pm, and were delivered immediately; they were dispatched at 8.15am and 3pm from the same place. By 1899 letters arrived and were delivered at 8am, 12 noon, 3pm and 8pm; they were dispatched at 8.45am, 10.40am, 11.50am, 4.15pm and 8.45pm. There was one person designated as a letter carrier in the 1840s and three by the 1860s. Later the Receiving Office was transferred to the Petersham Road [8].

CHURCHES

When the Domesday Survey (see p.4) states 'there is a church' this phrasing usually indicates that a church there had been restored, so it is quite possible, even probable, that there had been a church on St Peter's site since Saxon times. The oldest part that can be seen today, only from outside, is the blocked Norman lancet window in the chancel. Numerous additions have been made at various times [10]. There was some damage during the Second World War, restoration being carried out during 1949–51. The Canadian city of Vancouver gave a considerable sum towards the cost because of its close connection with St Peter's.

St Andrew's Church was built in 1832 [6, 7]; before that time the inhabitants of Ham had to walk or ride to All Saints in the market place in Kingston for services, baptisms, marriages and burials. Only those from the larger houses who could afford to pay for pews could go to St Peter's at Petersham.

Up to the Reformation, of course, St Peter's (q.v.) was a Catholic place of worship, but from then until the middle part of the nineteenth century there was no place locally where Catholics could worship. In 1856 a chapel, known as St Mary's, Ham, was set up in the grounds of Beaufort House, in connection with the private Catholic school known as Carrington Lodge (closed in 1870) but lasted for a mere 14 years, after which Masses could only be attended in Richmond or Kingston. In 1952 a site was purchased by Richard and Mary Cave in Ham Street, where Nos. 201–7 now stand, and a little Chapel of Ease of St Elizabeth's, Richmond was erected of inexpensive materials, with the intention that a more permanent structure should be built elsewhere later. The first Mass was celebrated in January 1953, with a congregation that overflowed outside. For the next 21 years, a weekly Mass was held, still under the administration of Richmond; people remember seeing Mr Secrett driving his cows along Sandy Lane as they walked to attend it. In 1974, after attempts to find a better site, the old Ham School (see p.19) was acquired, and transformed into the present Church.

A Wesleyan Methodist chapel was built in 1866 just on the Petersham side of the boundary with Ham, down the side of a narrow footpath, running down beside the 'Poplars' in Petersham Road (see map on p.30). A wooden building, with a corrugated iron roof, it was at right angles to the footpath, obviously meant to serve both Ham and Petersham. Services were held on Thursdays at 7pm and on Sundays at 11am and 6.30pm. Four people attended the first service, but by the end of the first year the congregation had increased to 24, with 54 children attending Sunday school. Vincent van Gogh, who was studying to become a minister of the Church, at that time a teacher and living at Isleworth, preached at the chapel in November 1876. The harmonium was played on that occasion by Miss Fitt, one of the two sisters who lived at Orford House (now St Michael's Convent) where they ran a boarding school for young ladies, and all the pupils were present [9]. After the first five years or so attendance at the chapel declined slowly, finally to such an extent that it closed in 1891.

All Saints, Bute Avenue began to be built in 1895 on the Bute House Estate by Mrs Lionel Warde of Petersham House. The Earls of Bute had lived there in a large house from 1785 until 1870. In the 1890s it was owned by Sir John Whittaker Ellis, who had been Lord Mayor of London and Mayor of Richmond. He put up the estate for sale by auction in 1895 as an excellent building estate.

Mrs Warde purchased the whole 21 acres to prevent this happening, thus to protect the View from Richmond Hill. Bute House was demolished, leaving the old lodge. As well as the church, Mrs Warde built a parochial room for Sunday School and as an Institute. She herself said that she was building for the future, for the time when the Sudbrook Golf Links would be covered in houses and other vacant land in the parish built upon earlier than was thought. She visualised this large church in the centre of a large population, with God there to receive his people. In fact, she was visualising Petersham as a suburb of Richmond. Fortunately Mrs Warde was one of those who helped to prevent it happening [12].

In 1928 the Ham Free Independent Evangelical Church was erected in Lock Road; it is now the only centre for Nonconformist worship in the Ward. In 1979 it closed, but has since been reopened as the Ham Christian Centre, supported by the Duke Street Baptist Church in Richmond.

With the development of the Wates estate (see p.27), a new Church to serve the needs of the expanding community became necessary. Part of the parish of St Andrew's (q.v.) was annexed and added to the area taken up by new developments to form a separate parish.

SCHOOLS

In the early years of the nineteenth century, only a quarter of the population received any education at all, while half the adults could not sign their names; their signature was a cross, i.e. 'Made their mark'. There were the public schools, grammar schools and academies for the better-off, but virtually no provision for the education of the poorer classes except the so-called 'dame schools', providing very rudimentary lessons for a small fee, and some charity schools financed by the interest of old endowments, donations and school pence [14].

The National Society for the Education of the Poor in the Principles of the Established Church was formed in 1811, schools that affiliated to it being known as National Schools. Whether a school was established at all depended upon the interest and support of local people who had to find the funds to set it up and run it. A National School was established in Ham at the early date of 1817, paid for by local subscribers. The children from Petersham who wanted to attend school had to go to the Ham School until 1849 when the Russell School was started (see below). Ham School was not entirely free — pupils paid $2d$. per week, two or more infants from the same family paying $1.5d$. Attendance was poor as pupils were kept away frequently, the boys to help with work in the fields, the girls to mind younger children if mothers were helping with the harvest. Indeed, it was not unusual for a school to close during the harvest as there were not enough pupils present to warrant keeping it open. In 1858, a Royal Commission found that only one person in eight attended a day school.

The Russell School was begun in 1849 by Earl and Countess Russell of Pembroke Lodge in one room in Petersham. A purpose-built school building was constructed in the Park opposite the Dysart Arms in 1852. Countess Russell continued to be associated with it until 1891 when it was taken over by the British and Foreign Schools Society. Thus the Russell school was undenominational, while Ham schools were Church of England. It was totally destroyed by a bomb in 1943. Rebuilt on the opposite side of the road, it is now a Local Authority School.

In 1870, Gladstone's Education Act doubled the state grant to existing schools, and set up publicly-controlled Board Schools to be paid for out of local rates and governed by elected Boards to fill in gaps and make a compulsory system. The prospect of having 'to endure the extravagance of the Board School system' was anathema to Ham. To avoid becoming a place with a Board School, they set about rebuilding the school premises, but despite this it became plain that it would not be sufficient to meet the Inspector's requirements. In 1887, faced with an ultimatum, a public meeting of ratepayers set up a committee to obtain tenders for the building of a new school, with the boys, girls and infants all on one site. It was paid for by local charities and public subscriptions with the help of the National Society. St Andrew's School (also known as Ham School) was opened in 1890, at the Ham Common end of Ham Street, built to hold 101 boys, 101 infants and 100 girls. Log books had been required to be kept to record attendance since the 1860s, but in the 1890s stricter rules were imposed; if attendance fell below a certain percentage, grant would be cut. In 1899 the average attendance was 70 boys, 72 girls and 71 infants.

In the 1890s, Miss Holland ran a private school at Elm Lodge, Petersham for those who could afford it; the fees were £2.2s per term in 1893, rising to £3.15s by 1895.

THE BEGINNING OF GREAT CHANGE IN HAM

The 1870s was the beginning of the shape of things to come, firstly in agriculture, then other uses of the land. In 1875 the main crops were still wheat, barley and oats; potatoes had become quite a large crop, with turnips, swedes and mangolds to feed the animals through the winter; small amounts of rape and greens had also arrived. Orchards, market and nursery gardens were small; there were 260 sheep. By 1895 the acreage of wheat had reduced by two-thirds, barley by 50%, oats by only a little, but peas, beans, potatoes and greens had shown large increases, and fields of carrots, cabbage and beetroot had appeared. Orchards, market and nursery gardens had increased by 400%. Total cattle had been reduced, while dairy cattle and pigs had increased. The area put down to grass had been reduced by 90% and there were no sheep.

Ham village was changing rapidly from a general mixed agriculture to a market garden economy, with crops being grown for sale, particularly to feed London. The better roads and more carriers' carts, as well as the railways (see p.12) made it easier to move fruit and vegetables to market more rapidly. Later, large areas of flowers were also produced. In 1908, a traveller passing along the Richmond/Kingston Road through Ham described it as 'acres of level farmland, bean fields, cabbage fields and a wealth of fruit. Country women were gathering runner beans in unfenced fields.' Land for roads and houses could be sold at a much higher price than it could be for agriculture or market gardens. One of the first roads to be built in Ham in the late 1870s was named, not very imaginatively, New Road. At this period it was not possible to give precise dates for the building of a road, for one builder would obtain a plot of land, building a few cottages on a row in it, usually calling them villas, e.g. Catherine Villas, Albert Villas etc. Similarly, other builders would add to them, until a road took shape. Changes in the line of the road, curves or bends, style changes in houses can readily be seen. Originally a private road, New Road was not taken over by Ham Council and dedicated to public use until the 1890s, when mains for services, such as sewage, water etc. were laid.

Evelyn Road came next with 18 houses round about 1884. Lock Road was begun in about 1890 along the line of an old field path as far as what is now Craig Road. There were only 12 houses in this road at the time of the 1891 Census. After the 1914–18 War a row of houses was built for returning soldiers; the road was eventually extended to its present length where it now meets Broughton Avenue by 1934. The 1890s was a period of rapid change in the structure of Ham, with more roads and houses being built, continuing apace in the twentieth century.

INNS, TAVERNS AND BEER HOUSES

There were three old inns, The Royal Oak, the New Inn and the Crooked Billet, while the labourers favoured the two beer houses, the Crown and the Fox and Goose. In 1861 a beer house was licensed as an inn and named The Hand and Flower. It is still on the same site on the Petersham Road, but the building is almost entirely of this century. In the part of Ham separated by the Park on Kingston Hill, and called Hatch since the seventeenth century, was the Robin Hood Inn, a very large one with room for travellers to stay for the night, pasture for horses and a farrier nearby; The Cambridge appeared in 1761.

In Petersham there was The Dysart Arms, which began as a farmhouse in the early eighteenth century, later becoming a tavern known as the Plough and Harrow. In 1804 the name was changed to the Dysart Arms. The original building was pulled down in 1902, and replaced with the present one, in mock Tudor style. The Fox and Duck is said to have been a coaching inn from about 1700; it was an old wooden building that had become dilapidated by 1940, when it was demolished and rebuilt. Locally it has always been believed that the original name was 'The Horse and Groom', but recently some doubt has been cast on this belief, and it now appears much more likely that the old Horse and Groom was at 215 Petersham Road, or maybe both 215 and 217, in the eighteenth century [H19].

SHOPS

It has already been mentioned (p.8) that from quite early times Ham was self-sufficient in the most basic items, particularly for an agricultural village. There were blacksmith and farriers for iron work and to shoe horses, boot and shoe makers and repairers to shoe people, carpenters to make carts and gates, and wheelwrights to make cart wheels. In very early times there was a windmill to grind the corn to make flour for bread. Most of these, together with dressmakers, milliners and tailors were not exactly shops but services. People could walk or ride to Kingston to the market for items that they couldn't grow themselves, while people from the large houses in Ham and Petersham would go to London for luxury items not available locally.

Shops in Ham tended to be scattered throughout the village, particularly along the Petersham Road from the New Inn, in Ham Street, in Boxall Cottages on Ham Common and 'in the fields', i.e. at the end of Back Lane. In 1839 there were three boot and shoe shops, a grocer, two butchers, a baker, haberdasher and linen draper; by 1845 there were also a Berlin and fancy shop selling wool, ribbons etc., a stationers and a second-hand furniture broker. In 1860 potato dealers and coal merchants made an appearance on Ham Common, along with a draper, grocer and butcher at Boxall Cottages, dairy, baker, shoe shop, two grocers and a carcass butcher along the Petersham Road [8].

In Petersham, in the 1800s, there were one or two dairymen, butchers and bakers, two boot and shoe shops, a corn and coal merchant and a grocers, scattered in Sudbrook Lane, River Lane and Sandpits, with the grocers on the corner of Sudbrook Lane and the Petersham Road. A few yards from Elm Lodge on the Petersham Road, a tiny Post Office, only large enough to hold about six people at most, was there until the 1870s. By 1879, Miss Long, the grocer, was also the Postmistress, with a telegraph office, and dealing in money orders. By the early 1900s John Keay and Son had the grocer's shop (he also ran a similar shop at No.1 Upper Hill Street, Richmond). After the Second World War this shop opened as a hairdressers, then a greengrocers, eventually closing in the 1960s. It was enlarged to form a private house.

When Ham's new roads were built, although the shops in the main were still concentrated where they were before, Holmwood Stores had arrived in Ham Street, a shop was opened at No. 10 Evelyn Road, a greengrocers in Lock Road, while New Road had a baker, general shop and a potato dealer; a dyer and cleaner had opened on the Kingston Road. Specialist shops came and went quickly, while butchers, bakers, boot and shoe shops and grocers stayed in the same families for generations — the Morffews, the Wiggins, the

Poveys and Hills. A copy of the Parish Magazine of St Andrew's for April 1915 has advertisements which may be of interest. These are not all the shops, but give a flavour of what was available:

PETERSHAM ROAD:

W J Hall	Hairdressing Saloon
R Morffew	Practical Boot and Shoe Maker
W V Povey	Family Butcher. Est. 1884. Families waited on
A Frost	Drapery, Millinery, Boots and General Store
G Rooke	Builder and Undertaker
A Hill & Son	Fancy Bread and Biscuit Bakers. Hot rolls every morning.

OTHER LOCATIONS:

A Holmwood, Ham Street	Grocery and Provisions
Winsons, Ham Common	Teas and Coffee
E J T Edwards, Ham Common	Milk and Dairy Products
D Lucas & Son, 12 Lock Road	Carmen & Contractors. Garden Manure, Mould, Turf, Loam, Gravel. Furniture Removal. Luggage to and from station
W Greenwood, Kingston Road	Families supplied with fresh milk and Cream from my own cows twice daily. Fresh Butter & New Laid Eggs.

The family of Warners, the wheelwrights, still had a shop selling wallpaper, paint etc. (in effect a DIY store) on the Upper Ham Road in the 1950s. The unmade road running down beside Barclays Bank to Dukes Avenue is called Warners Lane (though not signposted as such) as their shop was on the corner of the lane opposite the Bank.

NEWSPAPERS

Local newspapers were very late in starting. The earliest that included news of Ham and Petersham was the *Surrey Comet* that began publication in 1854. *Hiscocke's Notes*, an early form of newspaper, was a monthly from 1863 to 1868. Next came the *Richmond and Twickenham Times* in 1873, followed by the *Richmond Herald* and the *Thames Valley Times*, both in 1885. It is not really surprising that local papers came so late in the nineteenth century, considering the small populations in the villages and the standard of literacy of the bulk of the community.

THE VIEW FROM RICHMOND HILL AND THE LAMMAS LANDS

The change from an agricultural community that had begun in the 1880s was accelerated in the early 1900s by what appeared an innocuous desire by Richmond Corporation and the London County Council to preserve the famous View from Richmond Hill by a Preservation Bill. The LCC was purchasing the Marble Hill Estate over the river to prevent the Cunards from building houses in the surrounding parkland, which would be in the View. Lord Dysart saw that some advantage could be gained by joining in on the Richmond side of the river: he offered to help to protect the View by handing over certain areas of land in Ham and Petersham to be designated as open spaces for public use in perpetuity, free from all roads and buildings. By way of return for this concession to the public, he requested permission to extinguish Lammas Rights over a considerable acreage of Lammas Lands, i.e. the remaining common fields of which he was the owner. Lammas Day was originally 1 August, becoming 12 August after the New Style Calendar Act of 1750, the day by which the harvest must be completed. After that day, the Commoners had the right to graze their animals in these fields, even if they did not own a strip in them, for roughly six months of the year, until 6 April. Lammas pasture rights were the most effective way of preventing any new building. The Bill reached Parliament as the *Richmond, Petersham and Ham Open Spaces Act 2 Edward 7* on 18 November 1902.

In essence Richmond Corporation obtained Petersham Common (17 acres), Petersham Meadows (32 acres) and land lying along the Thames between River Lane, Petersham, and the southern boundary of the Borough near Twickenham Ferry, freehold from the Dysart Estates, the Corporation to maintain, conserve, regulate and manage. Ham Common (125 acres) was vested absolutely in Ham UDC, the Dysart Trustees also giving them £3,000 to be invested, the interest to be used to manage the Common, any money over to be used to improve almshouses or other charitable enterprises.

Sir Max Waechter, with no ulterior motive in mind, presented his fine house, Petersham Lodge, in River Lane, adjoining Petersham Meadows, to Richmond Corporation, to assist in the preservation of the View from Richmond Hill for ever.

The Ham Riverside Lands from between the north boundary near Twickenham Ferry and Half Mile Tree near the southern boundary was vested in the Surrey County Council, as it was agreed that Ham UDC was too small to find the finance to maintain them. No building was to be allowed in the parish of Ham in that part of the meadow between the southern boundary of Ham Riverside Lands and a parallel line 200ft from it.

Kingston Corporation was given a small area of 5 acres near the main road, further towards Kingston, suitable for a cricket pitch. All Lammas Rights on Lord Dysart's land were to be extinguished. At this period the Lammas Lands consisted of fields that for half the year were cultivated as market gardens, whereas for the rest of the year pasturage was little required, for in practice there was none. The theoretical rights were asserted by leading a cow over the lands; while these Rights existed Lord Dysart was prevented from using this part of his property for building purposes, and they did not enter into the View from Richmond Hill.

There was no substantial opposition to the Bill, which went initially to a House of Commons Select Committee, who passed it with only minor additions. There was nothing in the Act to prevent Lord Dysart from building on the Lammas Lands, yet he did not do so at that time. Instead he built up Church Road, along the Lower Ham Road and along the main road towards Kingston. On the Lammas Lands he leased areas to the Ham River Grit Company for working gravel pits.

AGRICULTURE IN DECLINE

There was still a large farm in Ham Street, the Home and Manor Farms having amalgamated by intermarriage, the whole known as Manor or Hatch Farm. Whereas the normal tenancy agreement had always been for 21 years, when F A Secrett took over in September 1918, although this was still so, there were restrictions. He was to carry on no other trade than dairyman and farmer, market gardens prohibited. Further, the Earl of Dysart could take over all or part at any time on three months notice, certain parts on one month notice and other parts on only seven days notice. Compensation was at the rate of £1.10s per acre. Apart from these demands, as more land was required for gravel pits, there were requests from the Ham River Grit Company for permission to construct a ropeway across the farmland or for land for a depot. By 1939 the tenancy was only renewed on a yearly basis. And so the writing was on the wall for agriculture in Ham.

Church Farm, on the east side of the main Richmond/Kingston road, that had been a large mixed farm with many sheep, was now a market garden and fruit farm.

URBAN DEVELOPMENT

Meanwhile, Lord Dysart continued to sell land for roads and buildings. By 1933 the first few houses were built in Dukes Avenue, together with the parade of shops on the west side of the Richmond/Kingston road; the West Heath School [H15] left Ham as they thought the village had become 'too suburbanised for a high class girls' school', moving to Sevenoaks in Kent, being replaced by the Lawrence Hall Hotel (later replaced by the Cassel Hospital in 1947).

By 1932 Parliament had decided that small districts must disappear. Surrey County Council proposed that either all Ham should go to Richmond, or that Ham Common and the old village part to Richmond and part round the Cellon and the Leyland motor works to Kingston. Both proposals were fought by Ham, but the second choice won, the boundary now roughly halfway between Half Mile Tree and Teddington Lock.

Petersham had already been taken into the Borough of Richmond in 1892. In July 1933 the Richmond part of Ham was combined with Petersham into a new Sudbrook Ward, with 3 Councillors [15]. Almost immediately Ham became an area for Council development, first by slum clearance from Richmond, then as the main centre for Council houses, Ham eventually having four times as many as anywhere else in the Borough, except Mortlake, and nearly double the percentage of unskilled manual workers (1981).

The population of Ham had remained fairly stable at 1,450–1,500 for decades, though rising to 2,200 by 1931, but once Ham became part of Sudbrook Ward no meaningful comparison could be made with previous population figures. Apart from the Council developments, building was also going ahead by Lord Dysart (Buckminster Estates).

In 1934–5 Buckminster conveyed land to G T Crouch Ltd for the building of Tudor Drive and the Tudor Estate. The building was to provide private dwellings only, except for professional residences for doctors and dentists, with prices and frontages all specified. The developers wanted to build shops too, with garages at the rear: the owners agreed, so long as no noisy or offensive trades were allowed. The mock-Tudor style parade of shops at the Tudor Drive end of the Richmond Road, east side, was built at this time.

There was a fruiterer on Ham Parade, along with a butcher, grocer, wine merchant, chemist, greengrocer, newsagent and Post Office, domestic store, ladies' outfitter, shoeshop, café and a circulating library. Buses on the 65 route were running from Ealing, through Kew, Richmond and Ham to Kingston every 15 minutes.

By 1940 Cleeve, Lovell, Mowbray, Murray, Riverside Drive, Sheridan, Stretton and the top part of Woodville Road had all been built. The ninth Earl of Dysart had died in 1935, his Estate being inherited by Sir Lionel Tollemache, aged 81. In 1948 he donated Ham House to the National Trust, and the following year the Ham and Petersham Estate of 350 acres was sold by auction in 124 lots.

In 1954, the award-winning Parkleys Estate was built by Span Developments, with Sir Eric Lyons as architect, on the land of Church Farm, of which the farm buildings (in what is now Ham Farm Road) together with their extensive greenhouses were destroyed by bombs during the Second World War. The other half of the shopping parade on the east side of the Richmond Road was built at the same time as Parkleys: the Parade was now complete. In the 1950s/70s there were two greengrocers, two newsagents and confectioners, haberdashers, wool and hardware shops, butcher, baker, ironmonger, ladies dress shop, shoe shop and at the Golden Acorn an Olde English Tea Shoppe. Between Parkleys and the Hand and Flower were a Master Tailor and a newsagents and sweet shop that also sold the type of groceries that people were likely to run out of: milk, bread, sugar, eggs, tea, coffee, bacon, etc. This shop was memorable, as it stayed open until 6.30pm, giving people time to buy a few things on return from work, the first local shop to do so.

Two dairymen, Secrett and Job, visited the new flats and houses to obtain orders for milk deliveries. Secrett had retained Manor Farm in the family since 1929, when it had 173 acres. As more and more land was taken for extensions to the gravel pits and for housing development by the Council post-1945, it dwindled to 60/70 acres; eventually it became so small that it was not viable. Secrett sold most of his cattle (40 cows and a bull) and gave up most of his land by 1955, continuing just with milk distribution in the area until 1957, when he sold up, moving to a dairy farm in Cornwall. The milk distribution passed into the hands of Hornby and Clarke, owners of the Petersham farm, the last left in the Borough.

Until the 1930s, there was nothing but grazing land between the last house in Ham, on the boundary with Petersham, and Lime Tree Cottage on the corner where Sandy Lane meets the Petersham Road. The developers, Park Estate, planned to build 18 mock Tudor houses, behind a service road, between these two points. By 1932 there was an estate in course of development between these houses and Sandy Lane. The roads had already been named Ashley Gardens, Arlington Road and Lauderdale Drive. On the other side of Sandy Lane, again grazing fields stretched away to the Copse. Meadland Drive, Clifford Road and Buckingham Road were to be erected, Sandy Lane widened and built up by the Richmond Council. 42 houses had been built on Sandy Lane by 1947, the final roadworks of the estate finished with Buckingham Road in 1954. These developments added a large number of houses to a very small village, but were not accompanied by any shopping parades or pubs. As most inhabitants probably know, the names of the roads Clifford, Arlington, Buckingham, Ashley and Lauderdale were the names of the inner cabinet of Charles II's ministers, commonly known as the Cabal. A nice touch; rather more imaginative than the current practice of naming roads by reference to previous Mayors or Councillors of the Borough whom no one has ever heard of.

When Ham Manor Farm House was partially demolished in 1958, there was found in the centre under the brick and stucco a fifteenth-century 3-bay Hall House, with hand-carved Gothic windows, leaded lights and one-foot-square oak beams, with partitions of reed, cow dung and sand [25]. Richmond Council built 13 new shops on the site, on the corner of Ashburnham Road and Ham Street, which never seem to have been in much demand, often empty and changing hands rapidly. Let us make sure that such an act of vandalism never occurs in Ham again! Ham Library was built on the Manor Farm Orchard.

The Council planned to follow this development in 1960 by replacing the semi-derelict postwar prefabs, on the adjoining Ham Close, with 9-storey blocks of flats. The opposition to tall blocks in a small village was so great that eventually 3-, 4- and 5-storey blocks, together with a Clinic and Public Hall, were built with the developers agreeing to provide a Green. 47 occupiers were to be within the slum clearance programme and 34 families on the top of the waiting lists.

The gravel pits had reached their maximum by the 1940s, and after the Second World War were gradually infilled with rubble and rubbish from bomb sites from many parts of the country [26]. This was finished by the early 1960s, leaving one large flooded pit as a lagoon, now the Young Mariners' Base. The Wates Estate of private houses was built on 60 acres of the land east of Riverside Drive. Together with the Ham Close buildings this was thought to have probably increased the population of Ham by about 3,000 in three years.

In effect the Wates Estate with St Richard's Church (see p.17), another shopping parade and the Water Gipsies pub turned Ham into two villages instead of one, joined together, and to both Richmond and Kingston, by the re-routed double-deck 71 bus route.

Later developments, apart from the Locksmeade development (see p.117) and Cowper Road/Beard Road, off Latchmere Lane were more in the nature of infilling, any open area being viewed with predatory eyes by developers, the large gardens of the houses around Ham Common being particularly attractive. The first to disappear was part of the grounds of South Lodge for Bishop's Close, followed by Martingales Close, built on part of the gardens of Hardwicke House, St Michael's Convent [H16] and a little of Avenue Lodge. Mornington Walk was built on half of the garden of Gordon

House, all around 1967/1969. In the 1980s The Orangery was built on part of Ham Manor House grounds, limited by the fact that the Avenue from Ham Common to Ham House is a Grade 2* protected view, and that nothing may be built to obstruct it.

Petersham suffered less badly, though there was infilling here also. Dickens Close was built on part of the garden of Elm Lodge, and other small developments were made in Meadow Close, Tree Close and a larger new development opposite the Dysart Arms, built on the Bute House grounds.

The rest of this book will describe Ham and Petersham as it is now at the year 2000; any account would be incomplete without a knowledge of how our Ward developed over the centuries. We have fought for our green spaces ever since we were deemed too small to be 'viable' on our own: history may make us wonder if there was anything that our forebears could have done over the years to make our area any different. We cannot afford another 'West Heath' exodus (see p.25).

COTTAGES ON HAM GATE AVENUE

PLANT 99

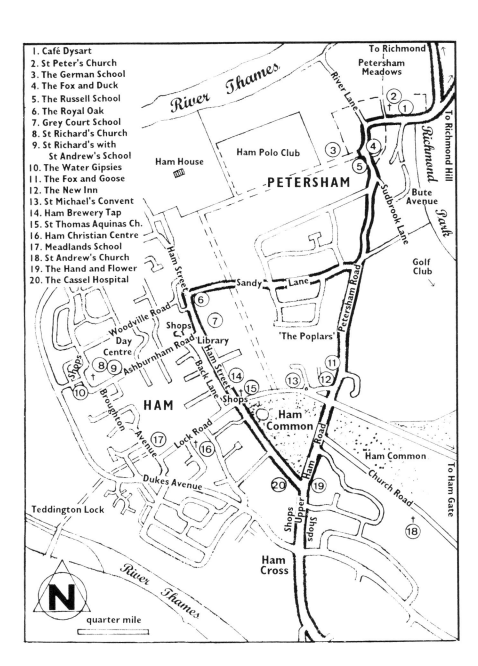

1. Café Dysart
2. St Peter's Church
3. The German School
4. The Fox and Duck
5. The Russell School
6. The Royal Oak
7. Grey Court School
8. St Richard's Church
9. St Richard's with
     St Andrew's School
10. The Water Gipsies
11. The Fox and Goose
12. The New Inn
13. St Michael's Convent
14. Ham Brewery Tap
15. St Thomas Aquinas Ch.
16. Ham Christian Centre
17. Meadlands School
18. St Andrew's Church
19. The Hand and Flower
20. The Cassel Hospital

River Thames

To Richmond
Petersham
Meadows

River Lane

Richmond Hill

To Richmond Hill

Ham Polo Club

Ham House

PETERSHAM

Sudbrook Lane

Bute
Avenue

Richmond Park

Golf
Club

Ham Street

Sandy Lane

Woodville Road

Shops

Day
Centre

Ashburnham Road

Library

Petersham Road

'The Poplars'

Shops

Broughton Avenue

Back Lane

Ham Street

HAM

Shops

Ham Common

Ham Road

Ham Common

Church Road

To Ham Gate

Lock Road

Dukes Avenue

Teddington Lock

Ham Cross

Shops

Upper Ham

Shops

River Thames

N

quarter mile

Geographical

Ham and Petersham forms part of the London Borough of Richmond upon Thames, bordered by the Thames and Richmond Park and by a wedge of green land that separates it effectively from Richmond proper. The only side on which its borders are in any doubt in residents' minds is that which adjoins Kingston upon Thames, in which parts of what was historically Ham now lie (see p.25). For the purpose of the current survey, only those areas that are in the Ham and Petersham ward of Richmond are covered; otherwise some of the information, such as that on the political, housing and population aspects, would need to be duplicated.

A walk along the A307 (see map on facing page)

The approach from Richmond is by two main roads, the A307 at the foot of Richmond Hill and the B353 coming past the Park gates and descending Star and Garter Hill. On both roads there is pavement on the right side only; at their junction are traffic lights that are activated by the buses to give them priority over all other traffic, and a pedestrian crossing. For a short way there is pavement on both sides of the road, but that on the left soon disappears. To the left is the Petersham (pedestrian) gate to Richmond Park; opposite this a narrow and muddy footpath leads around the Café Dysart and the side of St Peter's Church to the road that leads to the Nursery (p.104) and also to the footpath across Petersham Meadow. Further on., left, there is the entrance to a small estate built in the former grounds of Bute House (p.17). Pevsner's comment at this point is 'Petersham, for its small size, is unusually rich in fine houses of the late seventeenth and early eighteenth century . . . They lie close together at a sharp bend . . . and traffic makes it almost impossible to see them.' [27] The succession of distinguished houses has been covered in detail in [H16, H17]; road widening is impossible and traffic hold-ups inevitable as buses and large lorries fight their way through the narrowest parts of Petersham. A scheme for a by-pass through Richmond Park and part of the Golf Club's course (p.73) has been on the drawing board since 1935, but any attempt to implement it would meet with renewed furious opposition, and in the end only succeed in bringing traffic more quickly to the resultant hold-up on the way to Kingston. The sharp bend in the road is known as 'Tommy Steele's Corner', because that popular entertainer occupied Montrose House [H17] for some years. A little beyond this, in 1979, sewers beneath the road gave way; the A307 was completely closed for over a year. In the circumstances, the only way to reach Ham and

Petersham was through Richmond Park, kept open after dark to assist traffic. Now new proposals for closing Park roads are being considered (p.117).

At the 'Fox and Duck' there is another set of pedestrian lights, and the pavement reappears on the left. Just before this, on the right, a road leads past Tree Close (p.28), newish bungalows designed for older people, the German School (p.57) and the Polo Club (p.107); it continues as a path to the rear of Ham House. Just past Sudbrook Lane is Sandpits Road; along this stretch both pavements and road are narrow, making for unpleasant walking. On the corner of Hazel Lane, a footpath leading to Sudbrook Lane, a horse trough filled with flowers can be seen; the original, a product of the Metropolitan Drinking Fountains and Cattle Troughs Association, was demolished by a car, and a proper replacement could not be obtained. At Sandy Lane there is a third set of pedestrian lights and beyond the bus lay-by the pavement on the left again peters out; walkers have the option of using a wide pavement on the right or that in front of the row of detached houses built in the 1930s (p.26). Sandy Lane itself leads west to the 'Cabal' roads (p.26), the older part of Ham (pp. 8–9) and the Wates Estate (p.27). In this stretch of the main road, many car drivers increase speeds illegally, or indulge in bad-tempered overtaking, which has led to proposals to install 'traffic calming' measures. At 291 Petersham Road, ('The Poplars') there is an important landmark: the old boundary between Petersham and Ham, marked by a stone on the left (p.5). Just beyond this 'The Bakehouse' and 'Dairy Cottage' remind the walker of village days; on the left the pavement begins again by a large mock-antique house. Sudbrook Gardens, on the left, belongs to the 1930s. Opposite, a terraced house has acquired the sign for 'Ham, Surrey, Post Office' (p.21). At the crossroads on the Common (pp.9, 97–9) is the fourth set of pedestrian lights, a crossing for horses and the mysterious Ham obelisk [H20]. Here the pavement switches to the left again, though in dry weather it is possible to walk along the edge of the Common. To those seeing this area for the first time there could be a sense of amazement at how rural it looks with a large village green surrounded by fine houses and a few cottages, with the pub on the corner. At Church Road (p.9) a sign reminds us that there is to be 'No Dumping'; this injunction is repeated at the adjoining corner (Ham Farm Road (p.26)) with the added warning that there is to be no 'Digging of turf, trees, shrubs or plants'. At the corner of the road called Ham Common, that leads back to Ham Street, signs of village life mostly disappear, and there is dual pavement all the way to Kingston. The busy shopping area is then reached (pp.25–6) and eventually the fifth and final pedestrian lights at the Kingston border.   L C

A walk around the perimeter

'Beating the bounds' [8] was once an annual event in Ham and Petersham, though at the time our boundaries were less convoluted and far less built up. This ceremony took place once a year; ladders, planks, hatchets, billhooks and a pot of paint for re-marking boundary trees were taken. At each important boundary mark it was customary for the nearest boy to be seized and to have his head bumped on it. At the Thames boundary boats were hired. A walk of a less ceremonial kind around the perimeter of the Ward now helps to show what is excluded, and will explain what might be thought to be omissions from this survey. Beginning at the most northerly point of our riverside, the boundary cuts across a corner of Buccleuch Gardens, skirts the Petersham Road to the west, though a dip leaves a piece of Petersham Meadows curiously in the Hill Ward, then continues up the Hill at the back of the Petersham Hotel. A right turn takes us round the back of the Star and Garter Home (built on the site of the old Star and Garter Inn, where Dickens dined regularly [H13]). Another sharp left turn takes us to an oblique crossing of the Richmond Gate of the Park, which could well be called Ham Park since most of the land secured by Charles I came from Ham (p.7), and the greater part of the Park now lies in our Ward. There are views, to the left, of St Matthias Church, a favourite subject for local artists. The boundary carries on an irregular course along Sawyer's Hill, the northern road of the Park, but veers to the right before reaching the road to Holly Lodge (the administrative headquarters of the Park) to cross Queen's Ride and the Jubilee Plantation. Anybody trying to follow the bounds accurately would have had to climb over a metal fence from Petersham Meadows; their next obstacle would be wading across the northern of the Pen Ponds. The boundary now is much the same as the old Ham boundary [8] in a more or less west–east direction to the south of White Lodge [H10], now home of the Royal Ballet School, until Beverley Brook is crossed, when an irregular line southwards brings us to the main A308. Avoiding all buildings that overlook the Park, the boundary follows the Park's edge until a point not far from Ham Gate, where it turns west and has an irregular shape taking in Ham Ridings, Cowper Road, Beard Road and part of Latchmere Lane. Avoiding Garth Close it bisects the grounds of Latchmere House and Latchmere Close, leaving Garthside and The Shires in our Ward, and Barnfield Gardens outside it. All of Parkleys and the service roads behind the shops now lie in our Ward, but not all of Warners Lane, that muddy link between Upper Ham Road and Duke's Avenue (see p.22). The border passes behind the

Dysart School, then turns sharp left along the western edge of Dysart Avenue, which is still in Kingston, although Burnell Avenue, at its foot, once half in Kingston, is now wholly in Richmond. At this point the river boundary is reached.

Since the original partition of Ham (p.25) there have been complaints of the irregularity of this part of our border, and successive exchanges with Kingston have done little to simplify it. L C

The Thames boundary

We are particularly lucky in Ham and Petersham to have one of the most beautiful parts of the river to enjoy. In a walk along the boundary from just above Teddington Lock, with a small detour onto the footbridge (see p.38) to view the Weir, one might be anywhere but in London. Pleasure craft and the occasional gaily-painted barge are moored by the towpath. The bird life, which has become more varied over the past years, is described on p.90.

Progressing towards Richmond one catches sight of ancient steps, relics of the old Ferries, and along the landward side of the towpath the rich nature reserve of Ham Lands (see p.88). No sound of traffic, but in the background the roar of water at the Weir, and people enjoying the ancient pleasure of just walking. The quiet rural atmosphere has always encouraged fishermen along this stretch of the river, and more recently cyclists have also enjoyed this path, though the more aggressive and faster mountain bikers are not quite so welcome. Soon one passes the Young Mariners' Centre (see p.74) the entrance to which is on Riverside Drive. Next is Eel Pie Island, with its line of moored power boats; once the home of rock music, the hotel there was burnt down and has not been replaced. A more recent fire destroyed a number of craft workshops. There have been suggestions that a bridge should be built from the towpath to the Island to make foot access to Twickenham possible; there is strong resistance from inhabitants of the Island, who do not want through foot traffic, especially as they themselves have paid for the new bridge to Twickenham. Far worse was envisaged by the pre-war Ham Town Plan, where a road bridge near this point was included.

On the river bank opposite can be seen the steps for an old ferry below the White Swan at Twickenham, with attractive houseboats moored alongside. Such mooring cannot be haphazard; permission has to be obtained from both the PLA and our Borough Council planning department. A short way farther on, beyond the slipways at the Ham Street car park is Hammerton's Ferry, run by Stan Rust since 1987. Before him Sandy Scott ran it for 38 years, and before that Walter Hammerton himself for 40 years. Stan Rust's record number of passengers on a peak summer Sunday is 800. Sometimes he will extend his normal working day to bring back passengers after a Marble Hill Park concert, at night, on a dark and nearly silent river — magical! The Ward boundary veers towards the Surrey bank at both Eel Pie Island and the Ferry, leaving both within Twickenham. Otherwise the boundary runs centrally in the river, except at Teddington Lock, where it now extends to the opposite bank (see p.38).

The next glimpse of the past is of Ham House, with the restored avenue of trees up to the gates (see p.38) and the watchful reclined figure of a River God. The curve of the river beyond this is overhung by the ancient colossal trees at the edge of Petersham Lodge Woods; passing the entrance to the Sea Scouts grounds (see p.84) and the River Lane slipway one begins to realise that one is walking within the very view which is so famously preserved by Act of Parliament (see p.23).

Finally there is the herd of cattle grazing on Petersham Meadow: familiar yet always surprising (see p.100). Perhaps this is because of the sharp contrast with the busy Petersham Road, the steady hum of London traffic interspersed with the mooing of cows. This must be boundary's end!   C N

The River Thames
Most of the stretch which borders our Ward is tidal. From the sea, the first full Lock in the river is Teddington. Upstream from here is non-tidal, and a series of Locks is used to control the river flow all the way from Gloucestershire. Our final stretch of the tidal river is modified between Richmond and Teddington by Richmond Half-Lock, which operates for all but two hours before and two hours after High Tide. Three huge 32-ton sluice gates, hidden within an elegantly decorative wrought-iron double footbridge at Richmond, hold back the full force of the tides, retaining a deep almost lake-like stretch of river at Ham and Petersham.

Ownership and management of the river is very complex and includes everything from River structure, moorings and jetties, steps, and slipways to the actual river bank and towpath, navigation regulations, speed limits, registration and licensing of vessels, lights and buoys, control of pollution, safety and even ensuring that the swans are happy in their nests. The tidal river is controlled by the Port of London Authority (PLA), and upstream from just below Teddington Lock (marked by an Obelisk on our bank) by the Environment Agency. Richmond Half-Lock is therefore owned and managed by the PLA and Teddington Lock by the Environment Agency. These two bodies publish detailed guides, essential 'Highway Codes' for all river users, obtainable at the Locks.

TEDDINGTON LOCK

PLANT 99

All vessels on the Thames must be registered with the Environment Agency and the licence plates conspicuously displayed; from 1997 it has been necessary also to have a Boat Safety Certificate. The P L A is responsible for the registration of tugs and cargo-carrying lighters, but their current policy does not require vessels carrying less than twelve passengers to be licensed (this may present some problems with regard to smuggling, consequently a Customs Officer is a regular visitor at Teddington Lock). Vessels carrying more than twelve passengers must be registered with the Marine and Coastguard Agency, and comply with regulations for preventing collisions; they must also carry a Passenger Safety Certificate.

Maintenance and repair of river works and structures in our part of the tidal Thames is facilitated by an annual 'draw-down' when the sluice gates at Richmond Half-Lock are kept open over a prolonged period and the river allowed to fully ebb and flow. Structures which are usually submerged are accessible and can be inspected and repaired if necessary. At this time, the muddy foreshore, the full depth of the river and strong currents, which are disguised for most of the year, between Richmond and Teddington, become fully apparent. This picturesque meandering river can be seen to be powerful and dangerous.

A short section of the Surrey towpath, both upstream and downstream from Teddington Lock, is jointly owned with National Rivers Authority, but the remainder of the towpath at Ham and Petersham is the property of our Borough, which undertakes an annual survey of this public right of way. This is generally taken to mean clearance of obstructions and filling dangerous potholes. As part of the Highways system, clearance of rubbish is similar to other roads. Our Council has set up a River Forum made up of all departments which have a river responsibility, e.g. Transport and Highways (which looks after 30 of the 294km of Thames Walk), Leisure Services etc. The Forum meets with colleagues from the P L A, the National Rivers Authority and others and has produced a River Guide setting out the details of its commitment.   C N

Thames Landscape Strategy

Since its launch in 1994, Thames Landscape Strategy has drawn together various environmental agencies and Councils to guide the interests of conservation and heritage, public access, development, education, recreation, tourism and river use, at first along theThames from Hampton Court to Kew and now about to extend its activities from Kew to Chelsea. The Strategy evolved from a 1991 exhibition of ideas for London's river, organised by the Fine Arts Commission, which caught the imagination of local interest groups, to find ways of co-ordinating and enhancing the historic riverside, to work with to-day's users and nature conservation habitats. One of its aims is the restoration of local vistas, represented locally by the successful clearance between the towpath and Ham House.

Richmond Borough Council has been closely involved with the Strategy since the start, and indeed the Strategy head office is housed at Holly Lodge, in Richmond Park. C N

Teddington Lock and the footbridge

Teddington Lock, the largest on the Thames, is in fact three Locks, the central one being used most frequently; that on the Surrey bank is the largest, intended for barges, also used during peak Summer periods; the third one, which is narrow and deep (known as the 'coffin') is for skiffs. A total of between 14,000 and 17,000 craft pass through the Lock each year, the majority now being pleasure craft, either privately owned or larger pleasure boats coming up river from Westminster and Greenwich to Hampton Court; they cannot be boarded at Ham. There are still some commercial craft bringing commodities such as coal for the houseboats and Locks. More exotic cargo to Kingston has recently included all the glass sections needed in building the bridge from Bentall's to their car park , and the air conditioning system for John Lewis. A converted paddle steamer runs from Richmond to Hampton Court; its funnels remain, though no longer needed, and must be lowered to pass under the footbridge. C N

The footbridge was not always the responsibility of Richmond Council. Opened in 1888 (see p.14), it consists of two parts, a suspension bridge and a smaller girder bridge connecting to an island in the centre that is a quiet place for fishermen and for wildlife. From the island another small bridge leads to a long pontoon that accommodates some of the many private boats that moor in the area. The suspension bridge had to be closed at least twice as being in a dangerous condition. The most recent closure was October 1930–July1931, at which time Teddington UDC and local businessmen hoped that it would remain closed permanently and replaced by a projected road bridge. The Middlesex and Surrey Joint Committee on Thames Bridges thought differently, however, and judged that no further river crossing was required between Kingston and Richmond at that time. Repairs were then put in hand at a cost of £848 (less than the cost of a house in Dysart Avenue), financed by County and Local authorities, and it has remained open ever since. Were it to be closed again, there is now no ferry to take people across from Teddington to the island as there was in 1930–1.

In 1935 pressure from Teddington & District Chamber of Commerce, Brooklands racing track and Kempton Park racecourse was put on to Teddington Council to have a road bridge erected as mooted in the Ham Town Plan. The letter was passed to the Ministry of Transport and to Middlesex County Council, but fortunately for the peace of the area it was never built.

L C

Political

The parliamentary constituency is Richmond Park, covering that part of the Borough that includes Ham, Petersham, Richmond, Kew, Mortlake, Sheen and Barnes, taking the River as the dividing line with other parts of the Borough. Traditionally a Conservative stronghold, it was won by the Liberal Democrats at the 1997 General Election. The MP is Dr Jenny Tonge, who is the Overseas Spokesperson for the Liberal Democrat Group in the Commons.

Until 1892 Petersham was controlled by its own Vestry (see p.11), whilst Ham remained independent until 1933 (see p.25). The London Borough of Richmond upon Thames then controlled both villages, and with the reorganisation of Local Government in 1966, an enlarged Richmond Borough became the only one in London that controlled areas on both sides of the Thames. Since then there have been minor adjustments to our Ward at the Kingston border, tidying up boundaries, but still leaving certain roads in a half-and-half position (see p.33).

Ham and Petersham ward was represented by Conservative and Labour councillors until 1974, when David Williams (now Sir David, and leader of Richmond Council) was elected as the first Liberal councillor for the Ward, together with two Labour councillors. In 1976 a by-election brought a second Liberal councillor in, and from the 1978 election onwards all seats have been held by Liberal candidates. It has been a tradition that, with rare exceptions, they all live in the Ward.

The three current councillors are David Williams (who has lived since 1966 in both Ham and Petersham), Susan Jones (elected 1986, born in Ham, and apart from a brief sojourn in Kingston has lived there ever since) and Brian Miller (who has lived in Ham since 1980, elected 1998, though previously a councillor for Richmond Hill). Mayors during 1999 were Mary Weber and Michael Jones; in 2000 Barbara Westmorland became Mayor.

Conservative, Labour and Liberals all maintain local party associations.

Conservatives circulate 'Blueprint', a borough news sheet, periodically, whilst Liberals have a local free news sheet called 'Comments', which is delivered 5 or 6 times a year and concentrates very strongly on Ham and Petersham affairs. No other party keeps in regular touch with local electors.

Ham and Petersham forms part of the London constituency in European Parliamentary elections. In 1999 for the first time a system of proportional representation was in force, resulting in eleven members being sent to represent the large area concerned. The current MEPs (Members of European Parliament) comprise 5 Labour, 3 Conservative, 1 Anti-European, 1 Green Party and 1 Liberal Democrat members.

Twice a year, Local Consultation Meetings are held, usually in school halls at an evening time convenient for electors. These are widely publicised in the local press, in libraries and on the Borough notice board (see p.42). Local voluntary organisations are circularised in advance for items to be placed on the agenda; councillors attend to answer points raised, and there is opportunity for discussion and for raising questions outside of the agenda if time permits. Attendances vary; if there is an item causing local controversy, a large number of people will come. (Information supplied by Councillor Sue Jones)

Local Authority Services

Editorial note: The full range of these services cannot be covered in the time or space available, but some of the lesser-known ones are given in detail. Council income, of course, comes through the Council Tax, based on the value of houses, but although Richmond is reputed to be a rich borough, it is very short of funds, and the effect on our local services can be seen on pp.44–5 and 76. The comparative figures for adjoining boroughs as given in the Council report for 1998/99 are illuminating, and confirm the problems:

	RICH-MOND	KINGS-TON	WANDS-WORTH	HOUNS-LOW
Spending per head of population	£670	£723	£817	£966
(Kingston's population is about 40,000 fewer than Richmond.)				
Percentage raised by Council Tax	45%	34%	10% (!)	26%
Government grant per head	£148	£258	£508	£497

Mobile office
Each Tuesday a mobile Council office comes to Woodville Road, next to the Day Centre (see p.44), giving residents an opportunity to transact various forms of business and to save themselves time and postage. Council Tax and rents for houses or allotments can be paid, and information on all aspects of Council services obtained. It is at its busiest when the time for renewing Freedom Passes (see p.111) arrives, but at all times has a steady intake of visitors.

Recycling services
Throughout Ham and Petersham, large receptacles for glass, paper, cardboard, mixed cans and shoes and textiles can be found. They are unsightly, but perform the essential job of enabling those who resent the modern throwaway culture to recycle much of their waste. In addition, fortnightly collections of unwanted newspapers/magazines, textiles, foil and cans are made by a sub-contractor. Both these services lessen the amount of material collected by the waste disposal services and reduce the cost of transmission to infill sites outside the Borough. There is another positive benefit, in that revenue from recycled material is devoted to improving the environment; its local effect can be seen in the Gate House Garden (see p.95).

Social Services
Care at home for the elderly is covered under *Health and Welfare* (see p.45)

Removal of Graffiti
This is a service operated by the Borough Cleansing Department, and has already expanded from the original team of two to a second team. Their responsibility is borough-wide; recent publicity has tripled or quadrupled the requests for their service. The service is free to householders, but written authority is required before action can be taken. It is likely to be seven to ten days before this happens. Shops and commercial premises are expected to pay for the cost of materials used in removal, though the labour is free. Council properties, such as schools and library, are now covered by the service, but graffiti in open spaces is the responsibility of the Leisure Services department, which can buy the service to deal with problems, but whose budget does not allow enough leeway to pay for this.

Housing Office
Open Monday–Friday, this building, next door to Ham Library (see p.75) is

a collecting point for Local Authority tenants' rents, and provides opportunity for airing problems connected with individual rented properties. A Panel to represent certain areas exists (see p.86).

Refuse disposal

Collection of household refuse is made every week from whatever part of the premises (back or front) the refuse container stands. Householders supply their own plastic bags for this service. Shops and commercial premises have separate contracts either with the Borough Council or with independent contractors on a frequency basis that suits their particular needs, e.g. restaurants will normally have a daily clearance on public health grounds. There is an active recycling programme (see p.41). Sponsored litter bins are to be found around Ham and Petersham; a team from the refuse disposal section of the Council tour the borough every day from Monday to Friday to empty full bins; at weekends, however, they have to concentrate on Richmond itself.

Ham Branch Library: See under *Sport and Leisure*, p.75.

Schools: See separate section, pp.55–9.

Notice board

There is one 'community notice board' in Ham, and it can be found near the very edge of our Ward outside the shops in St Richard's Square. It is not there for notices *from* the community, but is intended to inform of Council meet-ings, Council services, and to give details of planning applications. It is likely that some people in other parts of Ham and Petersham are unaware of its existence; when its contents are not obscured by condensation it can be very useful.

Health and Welfare

On the whole, despite the damp and mists of a riparian borough, Ham and Petersham is quite a healthy place, though there have been medical scares in the past. In 1888 there was an outbreak of scarlet fever; several cases were removed from Ham to the Workhouse infections ward. A second outbreak of 33 cases occurred later in the year, of which 9 went to the infirmary. In April 1940 the Metropolitan Police asked that residents avoid the meadows adjoining Ham House, the footpaths through Petersham and the Common because of foot and mouth disease amongst cows belonging to Mr Smerdon, the farmer at Manor Farm, Petersham. The epidemic was also reported amongst the deer herds in Richmond Park, and straw was laid on the lower footpaths between Kingston, Ham and Petersham Gates as a precaution in case walkers spread the disease.

Ham and Petersham between the wars appears to have had no local doctor; Miss Landsdale's reminiscences [16] confirm this. In 1931 it was put forward as an argument for absorbing more of Ham into Kingston that 578 of the 590 insured persons in Ham were attended by Kingston doctors. A house built in Petersham Road in the late 1930s is now called 'The Old Doctor's House', indicating that a practice had been set up at some time. In the 1950s medical services improved steadily (see below).

Dentists

There are three surgeries in Ham and Petersham. The practice in Duke's Avenue has now been established for over 50 years; a service under the NHS is provided for certain groups of people, but the emphasis is placed on independent dental care. In Back Lane there is a partnership that serves both NHS and private patients; another partnership providing private care only is in the main road at the corner of Sandy Lane, in what used to be an estate agent's office (a *very* mock-Tudor little building).

The Cassel Hospital (Director Kevin Healy)

Since 1 April 1999, the Cassel Hospital has been part of the Child, Adolescent and Families Directorate of the Ealing, Hammersmith and Fulham Mental Health NHS Trust.

In-patient treatment is given in an Adolescent Unit, an Adult Unit and a Family Unit, within which is provided specialist help for children of the families in residence. There is also provision for outpatient and community service on referral from other medical services.

In addition training and consultancy services are maintained for individual managers, groups of professionals, institutions and for clinical consultation for medical professionals. Short courses on Management and Leadership in Mental Health Services are held, and fortnightly Visitors' Days for professionals are also a training feature.

A recent appeal for £600,000 has now reached its target; this has been used to provide a Families Unit building and to support research programmes.

The history of the building, described by Pevsner [27] as 'especially good' for its period, can be found in [H13].

The Lock Road surgery

Situated in a specially-designed building off Lock Road is a local partnership of doctors, who have qualified nurses to handle a variety of services such as wound dressings, blood pressure checks, weight checks and dietary services etc. Community staff attached to the practice are a district nurse, health visitors, community midwife and a clinical psychologist/counsellor; homoeopathic treatment is now available. The practice was founded in the 1950s by Dr Matthew Gardiner, and was located initially in his house in Lock Road. A surgery was built on part of his land in the 1960s, and later the house was demolished and replaced by a Georgian-style terrace of houses. With the growth of the practice, the new building was made necessary; while it was being constructed, consultations were held in the Ham Clinic (see below). The practice is part of the Richmond Primary Care Group and of Thames Doc, an out-of-hours co-operative.

Ham Clinic, Ashburnham Road

This is run by the South West London Community NHS Trust and acts as a base for the six District Nurses, two School Nurses and two Health Visitors. Doctors from the Kingston practice in Tudor Drive hold surgeries here most mornings and evenings. A chiropodist and speech therapist also attend, but by referral only.

Ham Day Centre, Woodville Road

This Centre, now that it accommodates a Special Unit for the elderly confused and those with Alzheimer's disease, seems safe from the closure that threatened it a short time ago. It caters for retired people, open Monday to Friday, and offering a range of services and activities including a hot lunch, yoga, keep fit classes, reminiscence groups, Bingo/raffle, singalongs with guitar, whist, organised shopping trips and summer outings. There are visits from a chiropodist and a hairdresser. Those who are too disabled to attend on foot are collected by a special bus that can accommodate wheel chairs where required. Each Christmas there has been a fund-raising bazaar, though the multiple clash of date that occurred in 1999 has persuaded those in charge to think in terms of a summer event in future. The hall is available for hire in the evenings; outside activities taking advantage of this include a Weight Watchers' class, the Multiple Sclerosis Society, meetings of the Area Housing Panel (see p.86) and the local Guide troop (see p.84).

Craig House, Craig Road

This is the only residential home for elderly people left in Ham now; there are two or three developments with Warden in attendance, including Red-knap House, but with the emphasis on Care in the Community there is less call for fully residential accommodation. Regulations on the amount of space required for each resident make it increasingly difficult to adapt large houses to such use, and even Craig House is under threat of being sold to a private company because of its need for structural alteration and the general trend nationwide of transferring such homes out of Council responsibility.

Craig House is far removed from the concept of a final resting-place for the elderly run on institutional lines. Its policy has been to create small lounges for six or eight people, each with an adjoining kitchen, both rooms serving a group of residents whose bedrooms are nearby. These bedrooms are mainly single rooms, with the opportunity to take a few personal possessions from former homes. The majority of the 36 residents are over 90, and many are incapacitated either physically or mentally. Because of this, and of the layout, it is not possible to lay on a programme of outside entertainers, though internally there is Bingo, and the occasional musical accompanist for sing-songs. The House also owns a small bus that provides local rides during the summer months. Admission is by referral from GPs, hospitals, or requests from relatives; an assessment is then made by a Care Manager, in case it is possible to provide care at home. (Information supplied by John Gray)

Ham Friends Club

Housed in a small building among the flats of Ham Close, the Club can ac-commodate 12 or 13 people in a relaxed and friendly environment. At one time funded by the Borough Council, it is now funded by Richmond and Barnes 'Mind', and opens on two afternoons a week. The activities include pool, Scrabble, music and the use of a computer, though it is not on line to the Internet yet. It is one of the least-known activities in Ham; should strangers ask how to find it, they are unlikely to obtain sensible directions!

Social Services for the elderly

Richmond's Social Services are controlled from three offices; our nearest one is in Sheen Lane. When a need is established, assessment is made and a regular pattern of visits established, including meals-on-wheels where appropriate. A careful record of progress is made by the Care Officers and the needs reviewed periodically. Equipment, including rails on walls to assist mobility, is supplied as required and access to doors to allow for wheelchairs can also be attended to. These services are available free of charge to the needy, but where personal resources are adequate a charge is made.

THE LOCK UP AND FOX & DUCK PETERSHAM

PLANT '99

Hospital

We are fortunate that at a time when hospital services have been concentrated in fewer and fewer locations, Kingston Hospital is within easy reach of our Ward, especially where accidents and emergencies are concerned.

Other services

Professional physiotherapy is available in Petersham, though not as part of the NHS. At the end of Ham Parade a bewildering variety of services such as facials, facelifts, treatment of scars and pigmentation, slimming treatment, cellulite treatment, electrolysis, sclerotherapy, aromatherapy & reflexology, permanent make-up, ear piercing, waxing and other beauty treatments can be obtained. There is a chiropractic clinic in Duke's Avenue. Aromatherapy can also be obtained at a private house on the Wates Estate, and Weight Watchers sessions at the Day Centre (see p.44). A private consultant for Stress Management, hypnosis and analysis also practices locally.

Animal health

There is one veterinary practice in Back Lane, Ham, established for over 20 years and attached to a long-established one in Kingston. It is open in the mornings and afternoons Monday to Thursday and on Friday mornings. Apart from the busy succession of domestic animals taken for treatment, squirrels, birds, hedgehogs and even a fox have been brought in; if their injuries are very minor they are treated and released, but most wild animals are transferred to Randall's Farm in Leatherhead, which specialises in such treatment.

Law and Order

By the side of the 'Fox and Duck' (see p.62) is a white wooden building that used to be the Lockup of Petersham. At that time Petersham's local police would have been responsible for selecting its occupants, who were more likely to be vagrants or troublemakers passing through than local people. A police presence in Ham during the nineteenth century was provided by constables, attached to Wandsworth, who were resident in the district [8]. Since then the only physical sign of the Law has been the small Police post by the side of Ham Clinic in Ashburnham Road; there was great local satisfaction when this was put up and manned, and even more when we were able again to see a community policeman on the beat. Sadly, both have gone with successive cutbacks in expenditure, and as this book goes to press the building is up for sale. Today we are served from Twickenham by patrol cars who visit the area regularly, and can be summoned with reasonable speed, but there is no constant local presence to inhibit the unruly.

Ham and Petersham (with Richmond in general) is probably unique in having three distinct branches of the Police force to keep order. At Teddington lock is moored a launch used by the River Police. Richmond Park has the Parks Police to keep order within the park; they have a Land Rover patrol and mounted police. Their control does not extend outside the Park.

A number of areas in Ham and Petersham have Neighbourhood Watch groups, with a coordinator from each road who is kept in touch with matters of concern to the local area by means of a Police newsletter.

Latchmere House Resettlement Prison (*Church Road*)

Latchmere House itself has a chequered history from its beginnings in 1808; this is covered in an article by Evelyn Pritchard in Richmond Local History Society's *Newsletter No.38*, April 1998. Local legend says that the Interrogation Centre of World War II, or Camp 020, had as its most distinguished 'interrogatees' Rudolph Hess and William Joyce (Lord Haw-haw).

The Resettlement Prison is the only one of its kind in Great Britain and attracts professional visits not only from branches of the Home Office but also from many countries worldwide. Prisoners spend the last part of their sentence in a manner that helps them to find their way in the community on release, but always under strict supervision and control. No prisoner with a history of sexual or arson offences is ever housed there. On recommendation for transfer, two Prison Officers visit the prison concerned to assess suitability; the final decision lies with the local Governor. Every care is taken to ensure thereafter that the dictum 'the public have the right to be protected' is observed; there is a two-week familiarisation period with risk assessment to make sure the prisoner is suitable, and thereafter a weekly assessment. Any breach of the strict rules leads to disciplinary action, either internally, or if serious enough by return to the former closed prison without the hope of returning to Latchmere. Once settled in, and within the strict framework laid down, prisoners have a degree of freedom, having their own keys to their individual rooms (though the individual buildings are locked at night), and being able to use what skills they have, initially internally as cooks, cleaners or gardeners. Afterwards they can be employed outside to assist in various community projects, mostly in Kingston, but locally at St Michael's Convent and the Cassel Hospital. They also assist in fund-raising for schools and, notably, at Ham Fair (see pp.77–8), where we have come to rely on assistance from a small team (though, like Cinderella, they must return when the clock strikes, to attend their evening meal).

The present Vicar of Petersham is chaplain to the Prison; there is also a Methodist and a Roman Catholic chaplain from Kingston. Members of any faith are encouraged to attend their own places of worship. The Prison staff welcome links with the local community; a club for 34 pensioners is run once a week, with members collected by bus or car, and the collection of birds of prey is displayed at local fairs and fetes. Interested visitors are very welcome by arrangement.   (Information supplied by John Morgan)

Places of Worship

Ham and Petersham has three parish churches, a Roman Catholic church and an independent Free Church. There is opportunity for differing styles of Christian worship in buildings that range from a small historic building with box pews to a modern church with chairs. For high-church worship, Baptist, Methodist, United Reformed, Unitarian, Quaker and Christian Science services it is necessary to travel into Richmond or Kingston. Two local groups offering a 'popular' style of worship meet on Sundays in the Hawker Centre, just outside the Ward boundary. Notes on Churches are arranged in chronological order of foundation; see pp.16–17 for historical information.   L C

St Peter's Church

From 1788 to 1891, the parishes of Petersham and Kew were combined, despite being 'inconveniently separated from each other by . . . Richmond', as an Act of 1850 puts it. Detailed information concerning the interior of the Church can be found in the pamphlet *St Peter's Church: A walk-round guide* and its history can be studied in Charles D Warren's *History*, held in Ham Library (long out of print). Its curious proportions are the result of successive additions made as the population of the village increased. Standing outside, or entering to see the box pews, large memorial tablets in Latin or English and high pulpit, it is easy to imagine that London is more than just a few miles away; Pevsner [27] describes it as 'a church of uncommon charm'. Holy Communion is said early on Sunday mornings, with a congregational sung Communion at 9.30 using the Alternative Service Book and Revised Standard *Ancient and Modern*. At 11.15 there is the rare opportunity of experiencing a weekly sung Matins, using the 1662 Prayer Book and the Authorised Version of the Bible. At this service once a month a choir, made up of a nucleus of parishioners augmented by singers from other Churches, sings the Psalm and an Anthem; three times a year, on Vancouver Day, Harvest Thanksgiving and Christmas Day, a larger choir is assembled, with a small orchestra; the form of the worship is then Holy Communion, with the choir singing a Mass. See p.69 for activities in the Village Hall, which is run and financed by the Church. The organ is a pipe organ, sited in the gallery, originally installed as a barrel organ in 1838, and rebuilt with two manuals and pedals in 1853 using some of the existing pipework. It was altered in 1914, 1976, 1981 and 1988; it now has a movable Yamaha console with useful storage and control features.

The large Victorian rectory in Sudbrook Lane was sold and a handsome new vicarage, matching the fabric of All Saint's Church (see p.55) erected. The vicar is the Revd Richard Bentley, who also acts as chaplain to Latchmere House (see pp.48–9). During summer months a group of volunteer guides ensures that St Peter's is open for visitors on Sunday afternoons. The *Petersham Paper*, a 4pp leaflet, is published quarterly.

In the churchyard the tomb of George Vancouver, one of Petersham's most famous residents, can be found. Other notable memorials are those to members of the Dysart family, whose vault lies under the chancel and the village war memorial.

St Andrew's Church. Built in 1832, the history of the building up to 1923 has been well documented in [6] and [7] both available at the Church, and deposited in the Local Studies Room. From then onwards, the number of parishioners has increased decade by decade, and there are still planning applications outstanding for small or medium-sized new residential developments. Structurally there has been little change since 1923, the significant new developments being a number of stained-glass windows and the recently-completed Improved Access project that not only enhances the area in front of the main door of the building, but also complies with the current National regulations for easy access. The interior is delightful for those who appreciate the traditional layout of English parish churches. Parish Communion is sung every Sunday morning, and Holy Communion is also said once on Sunday, on a weekday evening and Friday morning. Evensong, in the 1662 form, is sung every Sunday, and on the first Sunday of the month there is a full Choral Evensong. The choir is mixed, with a wide repertoire, meeting weekly for rehearsal, and singing at Parish Communion and also at Evensong. At Easter an appropriate cantata is sung and at Christmas the traditional Nine Lessons and Carols. The organ is a two-manual pipe instrument, originally built in 1903 by Brindley & Foster. The hymn book is

Ancient and Modern, Revised Standard edition. The living is in the gift of Kings College, Cambridge; at the beginning of 1999 the Vicar was the Revd David Moore, who moved to another Parish in Rothbury, Northumberland. His successor, the Revd Simon Brocklehurst, was inducted and instituted on 25 November. Other clergy are Revd Peter Lear and Revd Frances Forward. A Hall and Vicarage adjoin the Church; the well-patronised Hall (see p.68) opens out to the Vicarage garden which has been used by the Ham Amenities Group (see p81) for their popular autumn Garden Party over the past few years, and has also housed the Ham Horticultural Society shows (see p.86). Standing in this garden, it is easy to imagine that you are in a country parish, rather than a busy urban one. The present parish covers the area to the north of Ham Street, Ham Common, the Latchmere, Tudor and Royal Park estates and as far as Fernhill Primary School across to the river, together with that part of Richmond Park that includes Thatched House Lodge (home of Princess Alexandra and Sir Angus Ogilvy). A monthly magazine is published, the most substantial of any locally, containing full details of services, activities and advertisements from local shops and services. In addition to normal service times, the church is open to visitors at weekends from 10am to 3.30pm.

Twice a month on Sunday afternoons, a Lutheran service is held, led by Pastor Uve Wetter, and using German as the language of worship.

Ham Christian Centre.

From 1979 to 1998 no regular services were held here, but the Duke Street Baptist Church in Richmond have now renovated the interior at considerable expense to a very high standard. Morning and evening services are held each Sunday, the first preceded by a Prayer Meeting. Children's activities are held on Wednesdays (during school term times), as is a 6am Prayer Meeting. On Fridays, again during school term times, a club for under-3s and their Mums or carers is held, and a Youth Club for 12s and over. The Centre is self-governing, their Pastor is Mark Farmer. Set back from the road as it is, on the corner of Lock Road and Lawrence Road, built of red brick to blend in with surrounding houses, the building is apt to be taken for granted by local people. Inside is a hall, materials of which are of a high standard, with kitchen and another small room at the back. Music for worship is provided by either a Yamaha Clavinova (piano) or a 2-manual electronic organ with an octave of pedals and short compass keyboards; the hymn book used is *Songs of Fellowship*. The Centre exists 'to fulfil a purpose that is based upon the acceptance of Holy Scriptures .. to bring people to Jesus and membership in

ST. RICHARD'S CHURCH, HAM

PLANT 99

His family, develop them to Christlike maturity . . . in order to magnify God's name'.

St Richard's Church

The present parish boundaries take in the area bounded by the south side of Ham Street, the peripheral road around the Wates estate as far as Dysart Avenue, then north to Langham House Close and along the south side of the Common to Ham Street. Wates gave the necessary land, and early in 1964, in which year the foundation stone was laid, a hut was erected in front of where the present building stands. Soon it became too small for the expanding congregation, and was doubled in size (within a week); when the permanent building, designed by Ralph Covell, was opened, this hut was also demolished in a week. St Richard's was consecrated in 1966 and has become a centre of many aspects of the life of the surrounding community. The shape of the building is that of a star, and the interior, though lacking the focal points given by more traditional buildings, allows for great flexibility in arrangement. There is no Church Hall, functions taking place either in the School (see p.57) or inside the Church itself. In 1998 the building was adapted to provide a new kitchen, easy access and toilet accommodation for disabled people; further plans are for work near the entrance, to make the church more 'family friendly', when the required money is raised. The S.O.S service (see p.85) uses the choir vestry during the week; other activities are a weekly coffee morning that provides a lively social meeting place for both churchgoers and non-churchgoers, CAMEO ('Come and meet each other') meeting in private houses and Kaleidoscope meeting inside the church. Every year a piano recital is held in aid jointly of church funds and a nominated charity (see pp.79–80). Grass and trees surround most of the building; where the grass became worn away by being used constantly as a short cut, a permanent path has been laid during 1999 at considerable expense.

Sunday worship is traditional Anglican, using the Alternative Service Book and *Hymns Old and New*, which has replaced *Hymns Ancient and Modern*. There is a small adult choir; the organ is a one-manual pipe instrument with short pedal board. Holy Communion is celebrated at 8.30am (said) and 10am (sung) on Sundays, and said on Tuesday morning. In term time there is a Mothers & Toddlers Group on Wednesdays. A Healing Service is held on the first Sunday of each month. Vicar is Dr Paul Dunn (since 1998), assisted by Jenny Webb as non-stipendary curate. A brick-built vicarage in the style of the surrounding Estate, is sited nearby. Pamphlets giving more details of the history and furnishings of the Church can be found in Richmond's Local Studies Room. The church is open for visitors on Wednesdays 9.30–12 noon (3 o'clock during school term times) and on Tuesday 9.30–11am.

Community of the Sisters of the Church

This is an international Anglican Order, and the Sisters are familiar figures in the district. The full history of what was Orford House (later Orford Hall), is in [H16]. In 1949, the Church Extension Association (the charity under which the Sisters carry out their work) bought the house and grounds to become the Mother House and Novitiate of the Order. Of the 16 Community Houses in the U.K., Australia, Canada and the Solomon Islands, St Michael's, Ham is by far the largest, housing up to 15 Sisters. The Sisters welcome a variety of groups — for quiet days, parish retreats, prayer and meditation, as well as discussion groups and other kinds of meetings. In addition to providing space for groups and individuals, they also offer Quiet Days, Retreats and Workshops. In the early 1950s the house was extended, and a Chapel built, where the Eucharist is celebrated most days, as is Morning and Evening Prayer and Compline. Resident guests are welcome to join any of these acts of worship, as can others by request (except Sundays, as the Community encourages parishioners to worship in their own churches).

The Sisters seek to proclaim God's love to the world, directly or indirectly: through prayer, through the ministries of intercession, hospitality and Christian Education, and by ministering to human need however it is encountered. They also engage in a variety of creative activities, and are sometimes available to give spiritual direction and help with making a retreat if requested. Two Sisters are available for Counselling. An extensive garden, including a seventeenth century walled organic vegetable garden, 'Bible', and meditation garden is open yearly under the National Gardens Scheme.   (information supplied by Sister Valerie C.S.C.)

St Thomas Aquinas

Canon Davys was the first resident Priest when Ham was made a separate parish in 1987; the flat above the building was created for him before that date. On his retirement in 1992, he was followed by Canon Telford, who died suddenly in November 1997; the present Priest is Father Michael Clifton, also Diocesan Archivist. A Deacon, Revd Peter Simpson, was ordained that year. The history of Catholic worship in Ham is on p.16.

Mass is sung on Sunday morning and on Holy Days, and said daily. There is an adult choir that sings the Liturgy and an anthem once a month, also on major Festivals. The hymn book is *Celebration Hymns*. The organ is a 2-manual Bradford Computing electronic situated in the gallery at the West

End. See p.69 for activities in the Church hall. Every Sunday morning, following the English Mass, a Mass in German, for the large German-speaking community who live nearby is celebrated. The Porch area of the Church is open every day during daylight hours; a glass partition enables visitors to see down the length of the Church. A weekly newsletter, combined with the Service Sheet, keeps parishioners in touch with activities, plans and any problems that may occur.   (Information supplied by Father Michael Clifton: a full account of the Victorian Chapel has been deposited in the Local Studies Room)

All Saints Church, Bute Avenue
This red brick landmark , outwardly Romanesque, but inwardly laid out in Byzantine style, will remain, though closed to visitors. Its uses have been many; regular services were held there for many years; in 1941 it was requisitioned by the Army to house equipment to assist a local training school for radar anti-aircraft gunners. During the War it suffered bomb damage and stood empty until the Diocese restored it. The acoustics were so good that long-playing records by many distinguished musicians were made there and local concerts staged, taking advantage of the agreeable sound. Later, Greek Orthodox services were held, until that congregation found a permanent home in Kingston. Now it will keep its outward appearance, but inside has been converted to a private family dwelling. (Fuller details of the 'rooms with a pew' can be found in *The Times Weekend* of 11 July 1998.)

Education

Ham and Petersham is well provided with successful State schools for pupils up to 16 years old. It is home to one of the Borough's most respected secondary schools, three lively primary schools with nursery departments and a school for children with special needs. There are several privately-run schools and groups for children under school age, and a school in Petersham offering education to German-speaking families from a wide area. There are a number of courses and groups for adults within the Ward.   Gwen Dornan

Grey Court School, Ham Street (Headmaster: Mr Geoff Conway)
Grey Court began as a mixed secondary modern school with places for 600 pupils. It was opened in 1956 to serve the newly constructed Ham Estate, but has kept pace with the increasing local population and now has 1,019 pupils. In the mid-1970s it became a county mixed comprehensive school and has recently been designated a community school. Recent developments

include a new music block, giving the school an integrated arts complex; it has facilities for football, rugby, hockey, netball, tennis, cricket as well as a purpose-built gymnasium and a sports hall; the library has recently been refurbished, as have the Information Technology facilities. Pupils have access to a wide range of out-of-hours activities: field sports as well as individual sporting skills such as cycling and orienteering; orchestras, choir and instrumental tuition and a variety of interests from tropical fish to Duke of Edinburgh's Award Scheme (see p.87).

Richmond Music Trust uses the school premises for its Saturday Music School; Richmond Adult and Community College run evening classes in General drawing & painting, Spanish, Computer literacy, Body conditioning for the over 40s and Literacy and numeracy (basic skills). There is a close association with the local Tennis and Cricket Club (see pp.70-1).

The school is proud that it was recently granted Beacon School status, an award only given to the best-performing state schools in the country. The buildings incorporate Newman House, the only house in the Ward that has a blue plaque.

Meadland Primary School, Broughton Avenue (Head Teacher: Ms Tina Herring)
The school was built in 1952 to serve the children and families who were to occupy the new housing in Ham. It now has 7 classes plus a nursery unit and a teaching staff of 7 full-time, 4 part-time and 4 classroom assistants, led by the head teacher. The school is proud of its extensive playing fields, award-winning conservation area, activity centre and the separate play facilities for nursery and reception children. The pupils are able to take part in a wide range of out-of-hours activities including athletics, football, netball, gymnastics for the energetic; orchestra, recorder and instrumental tuition for budding musicians and also chess.

The Richmond Gymnastics Association makes use of the premises and Richmond Adult and Community College (RACC) is running courses for parents in ICT and Maths at the school. The school hall is also used for local Consultation Meetings (see p.40). Recent developments include a riverside mural in the school corridor, which was created as a community initiative challenge by RACC and local newspapers — and the children; the winning of a lottery grant for pergolas and sunshades in the field and plans for the creation of a web site.

St Richard's with St Andrew's Church of England Primary School, Ashburnham Road (Headmaster: Mr N R Brooker)
The origins of this school lie in the former Ham School (see p.19). The new school was part of the Wates estate (see p.27) and opened in 1966 to serve the many young families who moved into that development. It now teaches 181 children, divided into 7 classes plus a nursery unit, taught by 7 full-time teachers assisted by 1 part-timer and 3 classroom assistants. The school makes use of its football pitch and trim trail as well as an indoor swimming pool. Out-of-hours sessions are run for children interested in netball and football, drama and creative arts, French, German, and homework. In addition, local groups and the school's close neighbour, St Richard's church, frequently use the school premises, as does the Borough Council for public meetings.

The Russell School, Petersham Road (Head Teacher: Mrs Toni Richards)
The school's origins lie in the Petersham Russell School (see p.18). As their Millennium project, assisted by the 'Awards for All' scheme, a history of the school is being prepared. The Orchard Junior School was opened in 1951 and combined with the adjoining Petersham Russell Infant School (built 1954) in 1981. The history of Petersham Russell can be found in [H1]. The combined school now has 277 children in its infant and junior sections and 52 part-time places in its nursery unit. The school has a sports field, separate play areas and 2 gymnasiums, separate libraries and a science room. The children take part in sport, pottery, computers and chess outside their normal classes. Local Consultation Meetings (see p.40) are held in the school, and the Russell Robins, an out of school care organisation, also uses the premises.

The German School, Petersham Road (Director: Herr Köhncke)
Douglas House in Petersham Road was bought in 1969 by the Federal Republic of Germany for the creation of a school for Anglo-German families working in London whose children need to follow the German system of education. The Grade 1 house is preserved intact and is now used for school offices as a new building for the school was opened in 1980. Having started with 84 pupils, the school now has approximately 670 students of both sexes aged from 5 to 18. The school is housed in spacious, attractive buildings and has facilities for a wide range of sporting and cultural activities on site. The pupils learn English from the 7th class and the school is very interested in creating links with other local schools, by sharing the use of their swimming pool and other facilities. The school holds a Christmas market and a summer fete to which local residents are very welcome. It also acts as host to outside activities, including some concerts of the Richmond Concert Society, local

CHURCH OF ST. THOMAS AQUINAS, HAM STREET

PLANT '99

consultation meetings and groups from Richmond's twinned town, Konstanz.

Strathmore School, Meadlands Drive (Headmaster: Simon Rosenberg)
This is Ham's newest school providing full-time education. After some contro-versy over the proposals to site the buildings on, first, Ham Lands (see pp.116–17) and, second, the meadow behind Grey Court School, the school moved from Strathmore Road in Teddington to purpose-built premises in 1981. The School educates pupils aged between 3 and 19 years with severe learning difficulties. At present there are 28 boys and 18 girls on the roll, mostly from the Borough of Richmond, divided into 6 classes. The school has a teaching staff of 10 full-time with 15 classroom assistants. FOSS, the Friends of Strathmore School, support the staff and pupils. A special facility enjoyed by the students is the hydrotherapy pool, and this is also sometimes used by a number of outside groups catering for a range of ages: Richmond Back Pain Group, Richmond Health Care, Crofters Club for pre-school children with special needs, the Russell School Special Unit and 'Water Babies', a mother and toddler group. (See also p.107.)

Acorns Playgroup, Ashburnham Road (Leader: Mrs Helen Zandberg)
Acorns Playgroup has been part of the educational scene for many years. It began in 1967 as the Riverside Playgroup in Ham Hall (see p.69) and became known as Acorns Playgroup after it had moved to the old Youth Club building in Back Lane about three years later. When the wooden buildings were due to be demolished in 1983 to be replaced by St Mary's Mews the Group moved to share the nursery unit buildings at St Richard's with St Andrew's (see p.57). Acorns takes 24 children from two-and-a-half years old, using the premises in the afternoons; most of them move into St Richard's nursery unit when they are older.

Ham Nursery, Woodville Road (Leader: Mrs Georgina Llewellyn)
Ham Nursery also began life in Ham Hall (see p.69) and moved to its current premises at the Day Centre (see p.44) in 1982. It is an independent group, serving the local community and has places for up to 24 two-and-a-quarter to five-year-olds including children with special needs. The school is open from Monday to Friday and has six part-time members of staff.

Sudbrook School (Leader: Mrs Lynda Pollard)
The school began with only 6 children at Petersham Lodge in 1962. Fol-lowing a fire, Mrs Luddington, its leader, was offered the use of Petersham

Village Hall (see p.69) by the then vicar and the school was established there in 1964. The number of children attending is now approximately seven times greater, but the school still prides itself on its family atmosphere and often welcomes children from families with earlier connections with the school. The children attend from the age of two-and-a-half to five, and many then move on to private schools, including the German School (see p.57), or the local primary schools. The school is particularly proud of its successful OFSTED inspection last year.

Adult Education

There is comparatively little opportunity for Adult Education in our Ward. Two U3A (University of the Third Age) groups meet in private houses at present, one reading nineteenth Century novels, and one reading plays. The first has met fortnightly for over a year near the Common, and the play readings are done in a flat on the Wates Estate. A few classes are held at Grey Court School (see pp.55–6), and a highly successful WEA (Workers' Educational Association) group has functioned for some years (see below). The main opportunity for studies locally comes outside the Borough, at the North Kingston Centre, which is within easy walking distance of Ham Cross and also houses the Kingston Local Studies Room.   L C

WEA (Workers' Educational Association)

Ham Branch WEA was formed in 1970 and has been running Adult Education classes in Ham ever since. Some founder members are still active in the Branch as committee or class members. Class fees in 1970 were £2 (12 shillings for pensioners) and in 1999 are £56 (£48 for pensioners). Classes are arranged through London District WEA, who supply the tutors for the subject of our choice. In the early years the local branch ran daytime and evening classes at Grey Court School (see pp.55–6), St Richard's School (see p.57) and Ham Hall (see p.69), but in recent years we have run Tuesday and Wednesday afternoon classes only in St Andrew's Church Hall (see p.68).

There has been a continuous thread of History of Art through the years and the art of most periods from Early Christian, Byzantine, Medieval, Renaissance, Impressionism through to 20th Century and Post-modern has been studied. Other subjects have included Literature, Natural History, Local History, the River Thames, London, Tudors, Victorian, Aztecs, Ancient Egyptians and various aspects of Country House Life. Classes held during 1999 were as follows:

Jan–April   The Age of The Grand Tour (Tutor: Keith Miller)
              Looking at Portraits (Tutor: Chris Gatiss)

The Gate House, Ham Parade (Sarah Morffew's Cottage, 1771)

Ham Day Centre, originally the Infants' School

The Great Avenue to Ham House from the Common

Shops in St Richard's Square

Ham Lands

Shops at Ham Parade

Ham Library and Housing Office

The Tollemache Almshouses, Ham Street (1892)

Sept–Dec   Renaissance Art (Tutor: Keith Miller)
The English Country House and its contents
(Tutor: Chris Gatiss)   Freda Hyde

Public Houses

There are seven public houses in Ham and Petersham, many of which can be traced back for more than 300 years when they were either inns providing beer, spirits and perhaps accommodation and food, or beer houses licensed to sell mainly beer. That distinction has now disappeared and all provide a wide range of refreshment and other services with increasing emphasis on the sale of food and wine. All have a good choice of bar meals and several have full restaurant facilities. They are becoming increasingly popular on account of their more sophisticated culinary standards and ambience.

The history of the Public House is already covered virtually to the present day on p.20 and in [8], but a survey of their facilities and activities at the beginning of 2000 is the purpose of this section. Each Public House has its own particular tradition, emphasis and atmosphere and the landlord has his own personal contribution to make. The information that follows comes in the words of the landlord, and will help to give a lively picture of each establishment.   Bill Walters

The New Inn, Ham Common
This was known to be an inn in 1650 or earlier, and Martin McConn has been landlord since 1992. It has a warm and friendly atmosphere with good food and an excellent choice of beers (especially real ale) and wines.

Traditional cooked food is available all day and a traditional Carvery for Sunday lunch. To quote from *TNT Magazine*, this is 'probably the best Sunday lunch this side of London'. It received the *Evening Standard* award for best Steak and Kidney Pie.

Facilities include an open log fire and a Beer Garden with barbecues in Summer. A very popular event is the Quiz every Monday night at 8.30pm.

The Ham Brewery Tap, Ham Street
The new owners of 'The Tap' are Devonians, David and Doreen Wiggins who, having recently sold their previous location on the harbour at Brixham, have now refurbished the public areas to present an ambient, atmospheric Public House.

'The Tap' boasts two big screens to cover live sporting events, a 'Happy

Hour' from Monday to Friday 5–6pm with 50*p* off a pint of beer, live music Sunday afternoons and 'Karaoke' in the evening.

'The Tap' presents a 'value for money' lunch menu from Monday to Friday, 12–3pm, including their 'pint of prawns', 'The Tap Belly Buster', home made potato, leek and stilton bake for vegetarians, cottage pie, steak and kidney pie and the 'Plymouth pasty' (with a glass of cider), plus daily 'specials'. A traditional Sunday roast with 'real roast potatoes!' is served.

David joined the army as a boy in 1960 and having been commissioned from the ranks into the Staffordshire Regiment, he decided to join the licenced trade in 1985. He is a top rugby coach, and having coached in the army, in Devon, Exeter, Bristol and the South West, he is currently at Richmond helping with the re-emergence of that famous club. He is ably supported by his wife Doreen, a keen gardener and one-time marathon runner — hence her speed behind the bar!

The Royal Oak, Ham Street

Originally an abattoir for the farm which was across the road, this 400-year-old building has been trading as an inn for approximately 300 years. Some years ago there were two cottages attached to the side of the pub, and these were demolished in preparation for the widening of Sandy Lane, at one time a mere dirt track for cows which were led up it to graze on the open land.

Today, The Royal Oak remains very much a traditional public house with an 'olde worlde' feel. It is decorated with copper, brass and bric-à-brac and has low ceilings and low exposed beams, with an open fire to warm its customers in the Winter months It also offers a small intimate restaurant renowned for good value food with the emphasis on steaks, fish and some vegetarian options. There is a reduced priced three-course lunch for senior citizens. The pub stocks a wide range of lagers and beers, and has a comprehensive wine list.

Ken and Dee Blackadder have been at their public house for eleven years, and look forward to meeting and welcoming friends old and new in the 2000s.

The Fox and Goose, Petersham Road, Ham

A former ale house (see p.20), when the beer was sold through the window and patrons brought their own jugs, The Fox and Goose is tucked along the Petersham Road and uniquely in the village, specialises in the sale of Youngs' beer (one of the oldest and most renowned London breweries). Two houses were converted into a small but comfortable pub which also possesses a large secluded garden in which a collection of chickens and ducks wander freely.

The present landlady, Sue Clarke, has been at the pub for just over a year and is very proud of her entry in the CAMRA Good Beer Guide, the only pub in the village to achieve this.

The many house activities include Super League and Pub League darts teams and a cribbage team which participates in the Local League. The newly-formed football team is having reasonable success in its first season. All the teams hope to go from strength to strength.

In a variety of ways, such as a race night, a charity darts day and various raffles, the customers have raised nearly £1000 for the Princess Alice Hospice.

A number of events are planned for the year 2000, such as quizzes, live music, singalongs and trips to outside events such as horse racing.

Talent is sought in support of the various activities and Sue would like to hear from those who might be interested.

The Hand and Flower, Upper Ham Road

Built originally as a cottage in 1746, the building fell into disuse but was later rebuilt and became a beer house in 1848. Beer houses were simple labourer's cottages where thick and strong home-brewed beer was served to other labourers by the tenant. Inns, on the other hand, were patronised by farmers, tradesmen, craftsmen, carriers and suppliers; The Hand and Flower was named as an inn in 1861. It has undergone alterations, but some of the original features remain and the lancet windows facing the garden at the rear and on the north side lend a touch of antiquity to the building. The 'Hand' of the original pub sign is believed to be that of the Archangel Gabriel offering a lily, a symbol of purity, to the Virgin Mary as in twelfth century paintings.

In the days before mechanised transport, the patrons of beerhouses and inns would, in addition to the regular local customers, comprise a motley collection of foot and horseback travellers on the muddy or dusty roads, many seeking refreshment. They would have included inter-village travellers, hawkers, knife grinders, itinerant labourers and the occasional footpad.

Now the landlords of the Hand and Flower, Tom and Linda McDonagh, invite their customers to share in the welcoming ambience and hospitality to be found within these old walls, whether for regular relaxation, for celebrating a special occasion or as one of today's 'refugees' seeking respite from the stress of modern living.

The Hand and Flower is a fine old traditional ale house serving food every day, but where Sunday lunch is a speciality of the week. There is a very enjoyable session of traditional Irish music every Tuesday night. In the

Summer months refreshments can be taken in the award-winning garden, where the next-door neighbours, the Ham and Petersham Cricket Club (see p.70) can be observed enjoying their 'Teas'. It is not certain when this ritual began, but pub and club have enjoyed a cordial relationship over very many years.

The Hand and Flower is very sport orientated. Not only are all major sporting events shown live on TV, but there is a very successful darts team and a golf society that enjoys days out on local courses with all the trappings that accompany such a day!

The Café Dysart, Petersham Road

At one time the Plough Inn (see p.20), the present elegant building was until recently the Dysart Arms, but was converted to become as much a restaurant as a pub and run by John Slee.

John is very proud of its new image and says: 'Step across the threshold of Café Dysart and you step across continents and ages. In one of the most spectacular refurbishments in the Borough, the Corporate Catering Company has created a temple to fine wine and dining . . . quite literally.

'An eclectic mix of Baronial splendour, Italian palazzio and medieval ecclesia creates an atmosphere for entertaining friends, family or business associates in finest style or simply relaxing after work.

'For Café Dysart is whatever people wish to make it — local bar for that winding down drink after a hectic day at the office, a spectacularly romantic setting for an intimate dinner, a venue to do business in, or a refuge to take the strain when you have the children and the mother-in-law for a weekend lunch.

'When customers' eyes have feasted on the scene, they can tantalise their tastebuds on the culinary wizardry of John Slee and Arthur Przybylski. As the late John Denver sang "It fills up your senses" in a way that will have people coming back again and again. And there is a private function room so that they can have it all to themselves.'

The Water Gipsies, Ashburnham Road

This modern public house on the Wates Estate (see p.27) was opened in 1967 to serve the needs of the new development, and named after *The Water Gipsies*, a book affectionately describing Thames riverside life written by the late Sir Alan (A. P.) Herbert, who performed the opening ceremony.

The layout of the pub remains essentially the same as when it was built, although the interior was completely renovated after a fire in 1990. It has a large main bar with space to cater for receptions and large parties. In the early 1990s, half of the large car park at the rear was converted into a garden area, allowing greater freedom for small children to play and, of course, for clients to relax in good weather.

Now run by James and Moira Monaghon, The Water Gipsies has had many landlords over the years; its new owners are very interested in promoting community relations and in catering for families. At weekends they provide entertainment to cater for all ages and tastes; the atmosphere is warm and friendly. In the small bar at the rear they have installed a large screen tele-vision for the more sporting elements of the clientele, who also have the use of a pool table and dart board.

The Fox and Duck, Petersham Village

The Fox and Duck can be traced back to about 1709, but the present building was erected in 1940. It was taken over recently by Paul Martin and Paula, who were delighted by the scenery of the area and the friendly atmosphere generated by the local customers.

The pub has a wonderful open fireplace in front of which, with its crackling logs, many a passer-by has enjoyed a quiet drink in pleasant surroundings. A good selection of traditional quality pub fare is on offer, including delicious fillet and sirloin steaks, at attractive prices. On the last Saturday of every month, there is a 60s/70s night disco featuring the Classic music of that era, which attracts many people of all ages who enjoy dancing the night away. Also, it is a great place to enjoy a traditional Sunday roast, whilst listening on a Sunday afternoon to the excellent sounds of Bob Barter and his Jazz friends featuring Jenny How as vocalist.

Paul and Paula have plans to develop a pub garden with a children's play area that they hope to have completed by the Spring of 2000.

The Petersham Hotel, Nightingale Lane

In spite of its name, boundary changes have placed this hotel in Richmond Hill Ward. With the large hotels at the top of Richmond Hill and smaller ones on the riverfront it is easy for visitors to stay near to the attractions of our Ward; each is an easy and pleasant walk away from our boundary.

The Crooked Billet, Ham Street

The original building (see p.20) still stands. It was converted in 1924 to two shops with living accommodation above (see p.102); its replacement, on land opposite the Ham Brewery Tap, was demolished in the early 1990s and replaced by private housing.

PLANT 99

HAM HOUSE

A very small amount of bed-and-breakfast accommodation is available in the Ward itself. Two addresses are listed in the current Richmond Guide, and there are some others that are not registered with the English Tourist Board. But those wishing to stay and explore Ham and Petersham on foot are well catered for in the Richmond Hill area.

Ham House

The history of Ham House is amply covered in [28], and the contents in the official National Trust guide, both available from the shop. In 1948 Sir Lyonel Tollemache and his son Cecil generously donated Ham House to the National Trust, which holds the property in perpetuity for everyone to visit and enjoy. From 1948 to 1990 the Victoria and Albert Museum administered the house and worked hard to bring out the unique qualities of the place. The museum still owns the contents of the house today. The family connection, forged over 300 years of ownership, is of great importance to the Trust, and we are delighted that the present Sir Lyonel Tollemache has been able to furnish a set of apartments on the ground floor for his family's use. These rooms form part of the visitor route.

The Trust is keen that the local community should be involved with the property and enjoy its peaceful atmosphere. Many of our team of around 200 volunteers live in Ham and Petersham; without their help we would not be able to open the property to visitors. The volunteers undertake a huge variety of roles, from room stewarding, guiding and gardening to environmental monitoring, condition reporting and working in the shop. We have thirteen permanent members of staff, three of whom live on the property, and fifteen seasonal staff who work in the shop, tea room and ticket office.

Over the past decade, the National Trust has installed sophisticated systems providing the best possible conditions for the preservation of the building and its collections. We have also undertaken conservation work on much of the contents to ensure that it is preserved for future visitors to appreciate. The programme is continuous — over this winter, we have conserved the nineteenth century wallpaper in two rooms on the ground floor and have re-hung the pictures, putting out a selection from the reserve collection.

We are continuing to implement the garden restoration scheme, whose aim is to restore the gardens to their late seventeenth century splendour, complete with statues on the plats, orange trees in tubs and terracotta pots on the terrace. We have recently appointed a new Head Gardener who will be spearheading future improvements and have welcomed a fourth member to the garden team to cover the increased work load.

Funding a house and garden of this size is an ongoing challenge, as entrance fees and the income from the tea room and shop are not sufficient to pay for the upkeep of the property. Increasingly, we have had to seek new ways of financing the house and a more recent venture is the licensing of Ham House for civil marriage ceremonies, with the opportunity of using the rose garden for a marquee, or the Orangery, for the reception. We currently hold around thirty marriages and receptions a year, as well as playing host to a range of corporate events and concerts.

The National Trust aims to preserve the spirit of those properties in its care. We at Ham would like to think that, were the Duchess of Lauderdale or any member of her family to see the house and gardens today, they would still feel at home here.   Maria Flemington (Collections Manager)

Ham House is open from April until October, except Thursdays and Fridays. The Garden is open all the year round, with charge for admission. It can be approached very easily from the riverside, or through open land from Petersham. Pevsner's verdict [27] is 'externally perhaps not as attractive as other houses of this period, but internally of high architectural and decorative interest'.

Halls for Hire

Ham and Petersham has nothing in the way of a civic building; Ham Hall (see p.69) was built with that in mind, but for one reason or another did not fulfil that function. Without the Church and School halls, life for our local organisations would be quite impossible, and the variety of our activities would be very restricted.   L C

St Andrew's Church Hall, Church Road
In 1932, the Working Men's Club in New Road was renamed 'Ham Institute and Church Hall', and the Vicar of Ham, churchwardens and members of the Church Council became involved in its management. While Canon Beard was Vicar, this strong link continued (see p.78). The present Hall was enlarged after World War II, and contains a large room suitable for letting, together with a well-appointed kitchen and ancillary rooms for storage. There is an ample supply of stacking chairs and tables. It is very heavily used by groups associated with the Church, such as the needlework group and the Mothers Union, and houses W E A (see p.60), daytime dance classes for chil-

dren, an art group from Surbiton and an exercise group amongst other things. Ham Horticultural Society (see p.86) hold their shows here, private parties and wedding receptions take place. The Ham Amenities Group (see p.81) holds its annual Garden Party in the Hall and the Vicarage garden.

Petersham Village Hall, Bute Avenue
Built at the end of the last century (see p.17) the Village Hall is a substantial building with the possibility of being divided, and with kitchen attached. All parochial functions take place there, particularly the lunches that follow important Church occasions, and besides its use as a nursery school (see pp.59-60) it also houses badminton. It can be hired for wedding receptions, etc. Petersham Show (see p.86) takes place in and around the building.

St Thomas Aquinas Church Hall, Ham Street
Part of the old Ham School (see p.19), this Hall has become increasingly useful to local organisations over the past few years. It houses the Annual General meetings of both the Ham and Petersham Association and the Ham Amenities Group (see pp.81-2), the talks arranged by the Amenities Group, Ham Art Group (see p.83), children's dance sessions, an Irish Dance Group, and has housed meetings at short notice during the past year. An ample supply of good quality stacking chairs and tables is available. There is a small kitchen attached.

The Lawrence Hall, Cassel Hospital, Ham Common
The Hall derives it name from Miss Elizabeth Emma Lawrence, who was connected with West Heath School [H13, and see p.25] for many years. Over the years it has been used for a number of local activities, most of which have moved to other halls in the district. Now the main use is by the Cassel Hospital itself (see p.43) and the families housed there; conferences are held there, and activities for the residents. It can be hired for other approved functions, but no regular group meeting of any kind is held there.

Ham Hall
Built to provide a public hall for Ham's new developments (see p.27) the cost of hiring proved beyond the resources of some local voluntary agencies, though at various times it has housed WEA classes and nursery schools (see pp.59, 60). It now houses the Ham Youth Club (see p.87), who let it out to other users, including the Ham OAP No.4 Branch (see p.84), and The Wednesday Club for mothers under 25. The hall can be rented by arrangement with the Youth Club, not the Council's Education department.

Sport and Leisure

Sport has always had a prominent role in the area, some clubs having ancient origins. The sport survey, mainly by Jim Haude, includes some clubs that have gone out of existence, but nevertheless have made a major contribution over the years.

Ham and Petersham Cricket Club

Cricket has been played on Ham Common since at least the early nineteenth century. The first press reports, in 1855, give the name of the club as Ham Common; in 1868 it was renamed Ham Star, but the present name has been used since 1891.

Famous cricketers who have played on Ham Common, or have been connected with the Club in the past, include Sir Jack Hobbs, Peter May, Sir Alec Bedser and Sir Gary Sobers. Celebrities who have played include Roy Castle and Michael Parkinson.

The Club has always had problems through playing on the Common, with the associated difficulties of vandalism and storage of maintenance equipment, also the absence of adequate changing facilities. At one time players could change in an upstairs room of the Hand and Flower (see p.64), but these facilities became unavailable in 1965. However, enormous efforts in fund-raising enabled the present pavilion to be built next door to the pub on land owned by the brewers. It is a tribute to members of the Club that these difficulties have been overcome so that local people can continue to have the delightful spectacle of cricket on the Common.

Petersham Sports and Social Club

The cricket section of this club is recorded as playing Ham and Petersham Cricket Club before the Second World War. This club started life as a church team and then as Argonauts CC, playing in the Old Deer Park of Richmond. Activities ceased on the outbreak of war, but in 1946 the Argonauts restarted, still in the Old Deer Park. Subsequently the Club spawned a Tennis section and a Badminton section and, most importantly of all, discovered a beautiful but neglected ground in Petersham, behind the present Polo pavilion, the land owned by the Girls' College of Household and Domestic Science, Kensington. The land was on an annual tenancy, and all was well until the late '60s when the college was absorbed into London University, bringing various restrictions to the Club. Subsequently the land was sold; both the cricket and tennis sections folded in 1985. However, both

Clubs were resurrected in 1989, using facilities in the sports field of Grey Court School (see below); the Cricket section was, however, wound up in 1999.

Petersham Tennis Club

The Tennis Club in the grounds of Grey Court School (see above) is descended from the Petersham Sports and Social Club, but started virtually from scratch in 1989. It is now a flourishing Club with over 100 members, two men's teams and one ladies' team in the Surrey league. The Club pioneered a dual use arrangement with the school (see pp.55–6), and has a junior membership of 60.

Ham and Petersham Rifle Club

The early years of 1900 saw much activity on the part of Field Marshal Lord Roberts and others to establish a Rifle Club movement 'in order to strengthen the defences of this country should we ever be attacked'. On 11 November 1905 a meeting was held and a decision taken to establish an open-air rifle range for Ham and Petersham. In an incredibly short time butts were constructed and a pavilion built between what is now Riverside Drive and Ham Fields, and the Club was formally opened with a Garden Party in May 1906.

Famous visitors include King Edward VII, Field Marshal Earl Roberts, Lord Baden Powell, Lord Sudeley, the Earl of Dysart and many others, including many from the world of entertainment. During the 1914–18 War it was used for army training and over 24,000 recruits took their first course of firing there.

Over the years facilities have been greatly improved; the Club now has a thriving membership offering facilities in ·22 target/sporting rifle, clay pigeon, archery, muzzle-loading pistol and rifle, full bore rifle and air weapons. Over the years the Club has inscribed its name in practically every National Team or Individual Trophy in the sport, and probably holds a record for representation in international teams and the Olympic Games. The Club offers shooting facilities for scouts, cadets and other local organisations.

The Kew Association Football Club

The Club was formed in 1906 from the Bible Class of St Anne's, Kew Green. The Club has led a nomadic existence, never having a ground of its own; it left the Borough in the late '70s to team up with Richmond Town CC at Sunbury on Thames. The opportunity to return to the Borough came with the purchase of Ham Playing Fields by Richmond Council. In 1999 the Club received outline planning permission to replace the old and dilapidated buildings on the site with new purpose-built changing rooms and clubhouse.

The Club has a distinguished history, having twice won the highest honour in the A F A (Amateur Football Association) football world of the Southern Amateur league and the A F A Senior Cup. The Club has regularly won the A F A Surrey Senior title and were in the final as recently as 1993; their other teams have all won leagues and cups.

The A F A, of which the Club is a member, is the old governing body of soccer in the country; the ideals of amateur soccer are still adhered to both in that no player can be paid and that behaviour on and off the field of play is of paramount importance.

The Club has now expanded to eight Saturday adult sides, three Sunday youth teams and a veteran team. The youth teams have been added since the Club's arrival in Ham; with several fully qualified coaching members it is planned to expand the youth and coaching side over the next few seasons.

A note on King George's Field
This area, off Ham Street near Ham House, is owned by Richmond Council and includes tennis courts, football pitches, cricket pitches and a baseball pitch. Football pitches are let out on an annual basis, and teams playing include Twickenham Rangers, Kew Association and others.

Cricket pitches are used by Temple Sheen CC, Actors Anonymous, Teddington Old Boys and Kew Johns eleven. Baseball is played by Richmond Flames.

The Field is, therefore, used by various teams from outside Ham and Petersham, playing different sports. For many years Ham Football Club played here; it was formed in 1946 as a junior side (under 18s) based at the Ham Boys' Club in Back Lane.

The formation of a senior side followed and the club had considerable success in the Barnes and District League, Kingston and District League, Surrey Intermediate League and the Surrey Combination League, winning league and cup titles in all of them. Outstanding achievements were the unique distinction of winning the Surrey County Junior Cup in four consecutive seasons, a feat not equalled in the history of the competition, and, perhaps even more remarkable, the exploits of a certain Jim Punter, who scored a total of 270 goals in three consecutive seasons!

Surprisingly, support for the Club waned in the late '80s and early '90s, and the club went out of existence.

'The Fox and Goose' football team

Only recently formed (see p.63), their home matches are played on King George's Field (see above).

Ranelagh Harriers

The name Ranelagh comes from a district in Dublin and a family of Anglo-Irish peers, hence the title of Lord Ranelagh who owned estates in Putney and Fulham. The title is now extinct, but a number of roads and parks retain the name, including Ranelagh Gardens, home of the Chelsea Flower Show. Many sports clubs adopted the name, including Ranelagh CC, whose members founded the Harriers in September 1881. The Harriers is therefore one of the oldest athletics clubs in the country. Its first home was at the Green Man on Putney Heath, with runs on Wimbledon Common.

In the mid-1930s the Club looked for a new home, and found one in the form of an old pavilion at the back of the Dysart Arms (see p.64). The accommodation was rather primitive, and it was only after years of fund-raising that the Club was able to build a purpose-built clubhouse, opened in 1988.

The Club is a harriers club — that is, athletes run on the road and cross country; the Club does not have a track section of its own, but members do compete on the track of Richmond and Twickenham A C. The Club includes amongst its members many international and Olympic runners.

Grasshoppers Rugby Football Club

The Grasshoppers Club was formed in 1950. After several moves in West London they settled into premises behind the Dysart Arms (see p.64) from 1960 to 1974, using three rugby pitches in Richmond Park, but then moved out of the area to other pastures.

Richmond Golf Club (Sudbrook)

This Club was formed in 1891 with the acquisition, by the founder members, of the lease of Sudbrook Park from the Crown. The clubhouse, a Grade II listed building, was originally the home of the Duke of Argyle and was built for him by James Gibbs by 1728; its history as a hydrophatic spa can be followed up in [H17]. It is a private club with a membership of about 600, details of which can be obtained from the club Secretary.

On entering the course through the arch of the lodge at the end of Sudbrook Lane the view of the Palladian clubhouse at the end of the approach road is striking. It is probably one of the most attractive clubs in South-West London (Pevsner [27] calls the Club House 'enviable') and it has many associations with surrounding clubs, mainly on a competitive basis, all of whom are given a warm welcome when they visit Sudbrook.Reg Houston

Thames Young Mariners Centre

This was built 40 years ago, at the time the Wates Estate (see p.27) was begun and is owned and managed by Surrey County Council; there are three bungalows on site for staff members. Two Lottery grants have been obtained and used to purchase a fleet of sailing boats, new canoes, kayaks and two Dragon boats. Courses are not only for young people, although primarily the work is with children and young adults. Nor are courses confined to river skills; they also include instruction in First Aid, Diesel Engines and VHF Radio. A number of schools use the centre as an adjunct to their Personal and Social studies courses for the Team Building skills they can help to develop. The staff at the centre are all qualified instructors; during the winter season the Centre is used for internal instructor training courses.   C N

Playgrounds in Ham and Petersham

Children are fairly well catered for within the district, with a number of playgrounds and exercise areas, two in Petersham and one in Ham. By far the best is close to Petersham Gate into Richmond Park, fully enclosed and with a heavy gate which can be closed against toddlers making their way out and dogs making their way in. There are two wooden roundabouts (known in non-PC days as 'Chinese buses') and a further roundabout for younger children, four swings for older children and four for younger, a large sandpit with bench seats at either end, a log for climbing and a grassy mound. A seat is provided for parents to supervise their youngsters and a large brick shelter. Nearby are toilet facilities.

The other Petersham playground is at the Sandy Lane end of the Avenue to Ham House with an enclosed area for younger children containing an adventure climbing frame incorporating a slide, and four swings. Next to this is an open area consisting of four swings cleverly made out of old car tyres, a five-seater rocking horse and a 'Chinese bus'. A seat is provided close to the enclosed area.

The Ham playground is in Riverside Drive, close to the Walnut Tree Allotments at Ham Street. It is enclosed, with four younger swings, a five-seater rocking horse, three wooden swings, a wide slide and the usual 'Chinese bus'. Two seats are provided close by.

It is very gratifying to see that at the time of writing these playgrounds do not seem to have suffered from vandalism, unlike those in adjoining districts, though graffiti is now in evidence.

Some schools have private playgrounds for the use of pupils. The German School has a playground for small children adjoining the Tree Close footpath, with a wooden adventure castle and slide and, closer to the school buildings, an adventure climbing frame. Strathmore School has an adventure climbing frame and the kindergarten has a number of tunnels and a Wendy House. Meadlands School has a small playground, details of which cannot be seen from the road, and a wooden hut adjoining the school yard. Grey Court School has a large seating area near the Sandy Lane entrance with tables and benches which must be very pleasant in summer. St Richard's School has its own equipment bordering on Woodville Road.   Ron Chave

Ham Branch Library

Early in 1930, Ham UDC decided that Ham needed a Branch Library; they asked the headmaster of Ham School if he would be willing to run this, in addition to his normal duty, but on his declining, the matter was not raised again. After all, Ham UDC had other things to think of (see p.25).

22 years later on 6 September 1952, Ham Branch Library was opened to the public by Sir Compton Mackenzie. It was the first permanent library premises to be erected in Surrey since World War II, and held a stock of about 6,500 books. In the 48 years since this auspicious beginning this small village library has continued to thrive and has now become the focal point of the community. As well as serving the public with books, CDs and videos, it now holds a claim to fame as a library with an entrepreneurial spirit!

Ham Library Circle and *Ham Evenings* have both been set up to expand the minds, if not the waistbands, of the Ham adult community. In recent years the audiences at the events have explored a variety of authors, including E F Benson (and his world of Tilling), Beatrix Potter, William Morris and Dorothy L Sayers, as well as being introduced to some up-to-the-minute authors such as Katie Fforde. Musical entertainments have been provided with particularly 'rave' reviews, including our wonderful evening with, or in the spirit of, Noël Coward. This has all been done from the 'comfort' of Ham Library, and all with the aid of home-made cakes and beverages to provide sustenance to the stomach to complement the stimulation to the brain. We have also 'journeyed' to well known and lesser known environs: Hampton Court, Osterley, Selborne and Chawton, again without having to leave the cosy atmosphere of our local library.

For children expansion of the mind has been coupled with creativity of the fingers with some wonderful craft sessions exploring Egypt, outer space, Native Americans, Pirates and Japanese kites. These sessions have provided food for thought as well as an innovative creation to take home. As if this were not enough, Ham Library's recent history has also been 'peppered' with some incredible one-day events: Morris Dancing, D-day celebrations and Jazz bands have all been enjoyed within these walls.

As the year 2000 dawns, the Library enters a new phase of challenges and possible threats, but hopefully it will continue to thrive as it has a unique weapon: a close-knit supportive community that backs all its enterprises to the hilt and therefore enables it to go from strength to strength and weather the storms! Kim Hacker

Editor's note: Those who, on reading the above, may think that Ham and Petersham enjoy an enviable library service will be sad to know that on 25 January 2000 Richmond's Leisure Services committee cut the hours of most branch libraries by half, leaving Ham with one morning, two afternoons and a full day Saturday only. As a consequence, all but basic library services may have to be abandoned; the close relationship between librarians and community is now at risk, too. The storm of local protest has prompted a rethink, and a study into ways of keeping the present hours (already the victim of a previous cut), which could act as a 'pilot' for other areas, is being made.

Ham Lands walks

Ham Lands were transformed in 1972 as a result of 'European Conservation Year 1970', when it was skimmed with topsoil reputed to have come from M4 earthworks; tons of builders' and other rubbish was then removed. With the growth of population on the Wates Estate (see p.27), interest in the Lands boomed; local and national Natural History Societies took a serious botanical interest in the rich and diverse flora. In the European Year of the Environment, our Borough published *Ham Lands: A guide to nature conservation* [26]which as a source of information has never been bettered.

In addition to serious botanists, interested local people began to walk the Lands, noting and exchanging knowledge of species, especially the orchids and rarities. Its fame spread through my illustrated talks to various local societies, amenity groups and others who were prepared to listen. Regrettably, fear of walking alone in isolated places caused a decline in the numbers of walkers, except for those with dogs; an initiative by the Ham Amenities Group (see p.81) at their 1995 AGM established regular monthly walks led by local enthusiasts. These flourished for a time, but are now confined to special events by request. Summer parties from Ham Horticultural Society, Meadlands School, Richmond Ramblers' Group, Kingston Ramblers' Group, Friends of Barnes Common, Dysart Avenue Residents' Association, several local groups of the Holiday Fellowship, Teddington Lock Ladies' Circle, CAMEO (see p.53), The Richmond Society, Richmond Association for the National Trust, U3A (see p.60), Trefoil Guild for the Guide Association (and others) have been guided around, preceded by a winter talk with slides that I originally took for my own interest.

It is a delight that the popularity of these walks continues to grow; demand for them and for information concerning the Lands is as high as it has ever been.   Geoffrey Hyde

Walnut Tree Meadow allotments
Walnut Tree Meadow has the only allotments available to rent in Ham and Petersham. Allotments are run by Richmond Council Leisure Services, and are available at half price for residents over 60, the unemployed, disabled, students or those on low incomes.

In the late 1940s, the Dysarts were planning to give Ham House to the National Trust and to sell off most of their houses and land in Ham. Richmond Council had big demands for allotments as wartime 'dig-for-victory' plots were finishing. Also, and most importantly, there existed the Ham Agreement dating back to 14 April 1902, and set out in the Act of 1902 (see p.23) which decreed that 'the owner . . . of the Dysart Estates shall . . . if required by the council . . . provide land not exceeding 20 acres in extent as allotment ground . . . for the use of the villagers of Ham so long as there is a legitimate demand for allotment ground'. Up to 1951 such land had never been provided, but following negotiations culminating in a High Court writ, 13·68 acres were obtained, of which the greater part was given over to playing fields (see p.72), leaving 3·3 acres 'sufficient to meet the present and foreseeable need for allotment plots' divided into 48 allotments by April, 1955. The allotments came under the management of the holders, by means of an elected committee, in 1990; there is now a waiting list of 10 people. There is an annual holders' barbecue, held on the small area that has been laid out as a terrace with picnic tables. An Open Day was held in 1999. (Historical information taken from Dr Linna Bentley's pamphlet produced for the Open Day and available for reference at the Local Studies Room.)

Ham Fair
The Fair, in its present form, began in 1983, when at a committee meeting of the Ham Amenities Group (see pp.81) my remark 'We ought to have a Fair on the Common' brought the answer 'Good idea, why don't you do it?' Prior to this the Common had been used on a small scale for events to raise money for charity, but the 1983 idea started the Fair as we know it today.

The first problem was 'Where to start?', as nothing on this scale had been tried by us before. We solved this by sitting down surrounded by telephone directories and searching for charities whom we thought might be interested. This was not difficult, but very time-consuming, and to this list we added as many local organisations of interest, e.g. the Fire Brigade, Metropolitan Police, British Red Cross and local businesses. Having started we were amazed by the 'snowball' effect — suddenly we were getting enquiries from everywhere and the problem then became that of sorting the deserving causes from the 'professional' stallholders. However, a few discreet enquiries sorted this out and we got a reasonable balance of stalls. We then set about begging and borrowing things we needed, e.g. tables (Ham Horticultural Society and local schools) and of course raffle prizes from local businesses; the Fair then began to take shape.

When the Big Day finally came in 1984 it exceeded all our expectations and over the years it has grown bigger and better, mainly due to help from our membership and from the local Scouts and Guides without whom it would not be the success it is today as a source of funds for so many charities. Lady Annabel Goldsmith kindly opens the Fair year by year, and recently we have been fortunate to have Trevor Peacock, the well-known stage and TV actor, a former resident of Ham, to draw the raffle for us.   Reg Houston

Ham Institute (previously known as Ham Working Men's Club), New Road
It is surprising to find a building such as this in a residential road, yet many passers-by may give very little thought to it. It has been an important part of Ham, and has a varied and interesting history.

The land on which it stands was donated so that an unlicensed social centre and reading room could be built for the working people of Ham. It was very strongly supported in the early years, and provided a whole range of activities, including billiards, whist, bridge, an annual trip to the Boat Race, water and river parties, excursions to Richmond theatre and cinemas. In 1932 the Institute became the Parish Church Hall as well (see p.68), and the single-storey building was extended to two stories to accommodate the extra activities concerned. It is interesting to record that a drinks licence was eventually obtained with the aid of the then Vicar of St Andrew's.

Full membership is open to all men on approval by the Committee that is the governing body of the Institute; ladies can now apply for full membership. The building is open daily for billiards, snooker, darts and other games upstairs; downstairs the Hall can be used for events, and has a stage. It can be hired by members with the Committee's approval. A yearly event, still held, is a Christmas party for children. The Institute still thrives, and is by no means a 'closed shop' where new members are concerned. Its historical records perished in a fire that damaged the upper storey badly on 1 January 1953. *(Information supplied by members of the Club)*

Music in Ham and Petersham

It is unlikely that Ham will ever again have such an occasion as the Wagner birthday concert at Ham House in 1891, reviewed by Bernard Shaw, who came there by Twickenham Ferry to cover the concert for the *World* [29]. He declared that 'the Siegfried Idyll . . . has seldom been heard under more suitable conditions', though he was less kind to the singers.

In the past, singers have been well catered for, though none of the choirs concerned are still functioning. The *Friday Group Choir*, rehearsing at the Orchard School (see p.57) under Michael Haigh provided young people with an opportunity to rehearse and perform sometimes demanding classical pieces; this closed when its conductor moved to another school. The St Richard's School Choir (see p.57), formed and trained by the then headmaster Alan Dudeney, became well known through its radio and television broadcasts, and through recitals in such places as Southwark Cathedral, Portsmouth Cathedral and the Dome at Brighton. It gave a chance for the pupils, parents and friends of the School to sing a wide repertoire to exacting standards; with the retirement of the conductor it ceased to exist. Its 'Carols by Candlelight' in St Richard's Church was a popular annual feature. Another choir that had a successful life of some 20 years was the Apollo Singers, named after the Space missions and founded as an Evening Class group, providing opportunity to study and sing major choral works. One innovation that will be long remembered was their annual fund-raising supper concert, that usually provided lighter choral fare in a convivial atmosphere.

At the moment there is no choir or orchestra based in Ham; for two seasons the Thames Philharmonic Choir held rehearsals at Grey Court School, but now rehearses elsewhere. Ham needs a musical leader of some kind, for the talent is available locally. What singing there is takes place at the local churches (see pp.49–55); St Michael's Convent have just begun a small informal instrumental group.

In spite of the lack of suitable halls for performance (see p.68), there is a surprising amount of live music locally. The Richmond Concert Society stages several recitals annually at the German School (see p.57). In 1999 these featured a piano quartet, two pianists (one of them John Lill) and the world-famous Nash Ensemble. At St Richard's there is an annual piano recital in aid of Church funds and a charity by local resident Anthony Adkins, a former winner of the Chopin Fellowship from the Polish government. A concert was arranged in Hollybush House, Church Road, in aid of the St Andrew's Improved Access appeal (see p.50), and The Russell school brought a return visit of a Canadian folk group to our area. For the past two years the Ham Amenities Group (see p.81) has arranged an evening of music and prose on themes that have proved very popular with members and guests, such as 'The Demon Drink' and 'Spring'.

On a larger scale, touring operas and other professional groups are engaged for Ham House, and small groups perform at Pembroke Lodge (see p.95).

Television

Over the years, Ham and Petersham has been seen many times on television, and with its proximity to film and TV studios, coupled with the wealth of open space and fine houses, this is likely to continue. Some examples of past programmes are a black-and-white episode of Steptoe and Son, where its eponymous pair are seen driving in their horse and cart to see an old people's home (nothing less than Ham House!), 'Monty Python' filmed at Teddington Lock, 'Z-Cars' filmed more than once on the Wates estate, 'The Bill' filmed at the Water Gipsies (see p.64) and a holiday advertisement filmed opposite Ham Lands, when a house built of wood and paper was winched up to a lorry, leaving its tidy garden behind (the film company soon removed the unwanted plants, but left a few paper bricks as souvenirs). Residents of Ham Street were surprised to see Jennifer Saunders in an army tank being filmed outside their houses and the church. Costume drama has seen John Gielgud starring in 'Scarlett' at Beaufort House, and scenes from 'Longitude' shot at Ham House. Un-named stars seen recently were a kingfisher, caught by a cat but later released unharmed from Teddington Lock, and a baby seal rescued from below the 'Anglers' at Teddington, and taken over the footbridge to be treated at the RSPCA hospital in Putney.

As far as passive viewing goes, the saucer dish is evident in all but the most carefully-controlled parts of the Ward. Underground, Telewest Communications have their cables in most roads. They offer 69 programmes, on 47 channels, some covered by a basic monthly fee, but others (particularly sport and films) requiring supplementary fees. This may look to be a veritable cornucopia of entertainment; closer examination of the material on offer shows that sport, film, popular music, and hours of repeats predominate. Many programmes are of American origin, little is original material. There is one channel for Asian viewers. There are a number of specialist programmes, including travel, 'lifestyle', cartoon, or comedy programmes plus the inevitable late-night 'adult' shows. To achieve a balanced diet of viewing would mean a major daily planning exercise; past casualties have been the history and foreign language channels. A local channel covers news and events in our area. In 2000 a digital service will be launched, giving even more channels, and various interactive services.

Voluntary Organisations

Ham Amenities Group

At a meeting of about 100 local residents on 25 June 1979, the Group was formed under the chairmanship of Silvia Greenwood. Its main concern at that time was to maintain a high standard of cleanliness and tidiness in the area on both sides of the Common, organising regular litter picks and seeking co-operation with other like-minded local organisations. Over the years a variety of social events were set in motion with regular fund-raising for local needs and charities. In 1981 the Group arranged to purchase derelict land at the corner of the Common outside the Cassel Hospital to form what is now the Gate House Garden (see p.94). Ham Fair (see pp.77–8) was founded in 1984 and raises money for charitable purposes yearly. Ham Art Group (p.83) and the Theatregoers Group (p.82) are affiliated. The Group has continued to act to preserve the amenities and environment of Ham; a close watch is kept on all planning applications. Joint action is taken with Ham and Petersham Association on many matters. Membership is open to all, including those living outside the area, by payment of an annual subscription. Communication with members is by several newsletters yearly. Activities and finance are organised by a committee, elected at the November A G M.

A typical year's programme of social events includes four talks on a broad range of topics of general interest and four coach outings in the summer months, usually to gardens or stately homes in easy reach of London. In 1999, for instance, talks were given on tricks and puzzles, London's water supply and Kew Gardens at the Millennium. At one meeting, an entertainment in words and music was given (see p.80). The coach outings were to Scotney & Bodiam, Bletchley Park (home of the 'Enigma' project), Stowe & Claydon House, Hughenden Manor & Cliveden. Two or three coffee mornings and the annual Garden Party raise further funds for charity. The Group became a registered charity in 1982. In the financial year ended 30 September 1999 £2,450 was donated to 12 causes. In 2000 we celebrate our 21st anniversary; with the launch of this book also, we hope that it will truly be a year to remember.   L C

Ham and Petersham Association

Although Petersham became part of the Borough of Richmond in 1892, Ham was independent (see p.25) until 1933, when the Sudbrook Ward Ratepayers' Association was formed because of the fears of lack of full representation on the Council. This later became the Ham and Petersham Ratepayers' Association (later still the title 'and Residents' was added), taking its present title when the rating system was replaced in 1989.

The aim of the Association is to protect the special environment of Ham and Petersham and the interests of its residents. An elected committee meets on a regular basis to pursue these aims. The majority of its work has been to prevent the development and exploitation of the open spaces and to ensure that new building does not cause visual disturbance or loss of amenity. This involves close monitoring of all local planning applications.

The Association's work at the turn of the century continues with such controversial issues as increased traffic and parking, the proposed closure of Richmond Park to through traffic, vandalism, graffiti, litter as well as inappropriate notices and signs. The Association seeks to influence Richmond Council's policy in properly maintaining the open spaces, footpaths, avenues and to ensure that the Council does not permit the misuse of public land. It has also been very involved in seeking ways to preserve the Petersham Meadows.

Today, membership (currently around 600) is open to all who live in Ham and Petersham, with an annual subscription of £3 per person. There is an annual summer garden party held at Ham House, which is much enjoyed by members and friends.   Sylvia Peile

Theatregoers Group

A flourishing offshoot of the Ham Amenities Group (see p.81), affiliated to the Theatregoers' Club of Great Britain. Members receive advance notice of a wide variety of entertainments in the West End, and also regional venues. Accompanied by the Area Manager (Sue James), theatregoers travel in a comfortable coach from convenient pick-up points. The facility takes the sting out of theatregoing and avoids parking or public transport problems. Day excursions include river cruises, visits to stately homes and museums. On many of these excursions excellent meals are included. Memorable outings have included a guided tour of the Houses of Parliament, Buckingham Palace and Kensington Palace, Woburn Abbey and to the *Monet in the Twentieth Century* exhibition at the Royal Academy.

Members have enjoyed a wide range of plays and musicals (including *Chicago, Oklahoma* and *The Lion King*), the Royal Ballet, Chichester

Festival Theatre, The Mill at Sonning and carols at the Royal Festival Hall.

A highlight early in 2000 was a river cruise to the Dome on board the former Dutch Royal Yacht, with sumptuous lunching on board, three hours in the Dome and a grand finale featuring the exclusive lifting of Tower Bridge on the return journey.

Local members meet and introduce friends at coffee morning, held at the New Inn (see pp. 61–2) on the first Thursday of the month. These informal gatherings give opportunities to make new friends with a shared interest in the arts. Theatre holidays in the UK and world wide can be arranged.

Cecily Doughty and Sue James

Ham Art Group

Started by the Ham Amenities Group (see p.81), this continues to prosper. It now has some 36 members, but there is a limit on membership due to space available in St Thomas Aquinas Hall (see p.69). There continues to be a waiting list which is a healthy sign, although frustrating to those wishing to join.

The Group meets on Wednesdays from 10am to 4pm with many bringing a packed lunch to eat with others in the Hall around 12.30pm. These lunchtime sessions give a lively social focus to the Group. It is a workshop where members work individually; there is no tuition and no commercial demonstrations are planned for the year 2000. There are three terms of twelve weeks' duration, the fee being £10 per term.

The Annual Exhibition continues to arouse local interest although, as with other amateur art clubs, sales are declining. In the 1999 exhibition 15 works were sold, but more successful was the one at Pembroke Lodge (see p.95), where visitors came from afar and 28 pictures were sold, some to visitors from overseas.

In 2000 the Annual Exhibition will be held over the Spring Bank holiday, with a private view for invited guests on the Friday evening. The private view is a pleasant social occasion for members and their friends to meet each other over a glass of wine and to show off their works. It is planned, as usual, to hold a small exhibition in part of a marquee at Ham Fair (see pp.77–8), but we do not expect to sell many works there. A 7-day exhibition will again be mounted at Pembroke Lodge, but this year it has to be held in October instead of during the August bank holiday as in previous years. In October St Richard's Church (see p.53) are holding an Art festival, and have invited our members to participate. The year will end with the usual Christmas Party on the last day of term, where members bring food and invite their friends.

John Seager

Scouting and Guiding

Ham Scout Group was formed around 1945, drawing many early members from the choir of St Andrew's Church (see pp.50–1). Early meetings were held in the Church Vestry, then in Ham School (see p.19), followed by Grey Court School. The Group eventually moved into its own Headquarters in the Avenue, built by group members, parents and friends under the inspiration and guidance of an early Group Scout Leader, Michael (Tig) Hymas.

Ham & Petersham District Guide Association was formed in 1925, when the 1st Ham Common and 7th Richmond companies were re-registered as Ham & Petersham District. Meetings were held in all the local schools before 1983, when the District acquired its own Headquarters in Woodville Road, Ham (formerly the Ham Infants School), thanks to the vision and inspiration of Wendy Holwill, who was District Commissioner at the time. Close links are maintained with St Richard's Church today, some units being affiliated to the Church.

To achieve the aims of Scouting and Guiding, activities and training are provided for children in the local area within a world-wide movement, encouraging teamwork and friendship, commitment to the local community and having fun together! The Scouts and Guides have participated in a wide range of activities over the years, with joint ventures featuring prominently in recent times, expeditions to Norway and America being especially memorable.

Scouts offer activities and training for Beavers (aged 6–8), Cubs (8–10), Scouts (10–15) and Venture Scouts (15–21); the Guides provide similar opportunities for Rainbows (5–7), Brownies (7–10), Guides (10–16) and Senior Section (14–26).   Deborah Blakemore (District
Commissioner, Ham & Petersham District Guide Association)
Michael Holwill (Group Scout Leader, Ham Scout Group)

The 12th Kingston (St Andrew's) Guides and Brownies meet outside our Ward, but are attached to one of our parish churches.

Petersham and Ham Sea Scouts (Admiralty recognised)

This takes children and young people of both sexes. Founded in 1908, its headquarters are in Douglas House Meadow, where Beavers (aged 6–8 years), Cubs (8–10) and Scouts (10–15) hold weekly meetings. Ventures (15–20) have special arrangements for meetings. During the weekly meetings the Scouts learn useful skills such as working in teams, sharing and making friends. The older ones have activities based on practical skills such as map reading, first aid and seamanship.

Special events are: swimming gala at HMS Raleigh in Plymouth for Admiralty recognised troops, visits to Scotland and international Jamborees, and taking part in the Great River Race. Karin Noble

Ham and Petersham SOS

This is a neighbourhood care scheme run entirely by volunteers for the benefit of all in our community. It was founded in the mid-1960s by some of the first residents of the Wates Estate who, with few cars and (at that time) a poor bus service, helped each other out with lifts to doctors, dentists, clinics, hospitals or the shops.

Soon the service extended to cover the whole of Ham and Petersham, became affiliated to Richmond CVS (Council for Voluntary Service), and started getting referrals from the statutory bodies (Health Authorities and Social Services). In the early 1980s an office was set up in St Richard's Church (see p.53) on weekday mornings where phone organisers could receive requests for help and contact the volunteers.

The service now deals with approximately 1500 requests annually and has extended its range to cover simple DIY jobs, shopping and visiting the housebound. A pool of 40–50 volunteers aged between 35 and 90 help as often as they wish (anything from once a year to three times a week). Thanks to the generosity of clients and other groups in the community it is self-financing, though drivers may claim petrol allowances from Richmond CVS.

The prospect of further pressure on Social Services and on the family as a social unit can only mean a continuing and increasing need for our SOS in the twenty-first century. It is to be hoped that when the present volunteers themselves become clients there will be others prepared to step into their shoes. Angela Roberts

Ham and Petersham Old Age Pensioners' Association, Branch No.4

This is one of the hidden features of our Ward: its good work attracts little publicity, and it does not advertise itself. Branches Nos. 2 and 3 no longer function; Branch No.1 is reputed to exist, but resists discovery.

The Association is governed by an elected committee, and in the past has received a measure of Council funding that covers part of the rent of halls. Once a week a Bingo session is held in Ham Hall (see p.69); during the summer seaside outings are organised and at Christmas a party is held, though as a departure for 1999 an excursion to see the lights and a fish-and-chips supper was held. At Easter and on anniversaries of formation, special celebrations are held. The committee raises funds to cover the cost of these.

Volunteers at Ham House

There are over 200 volunteers at Ham House (see p.66), recruited from the local community and from farther afield. They undertake a great variety of roles, of which the principal duty is room stewarding, while the house is open to the public. Annual training sessions are given to bring everyone up to date with changes on the property, and the House offers a lecture series, as well as an outing and social events.   M F

Ham Area Housing Panel

This is an elected body, drawn from the three functioning Residents' Associations covering Local Authority rented property. The three areas concerned are (1) Ham Close, (2) Beaufort Court (3) Ham Green South. Meetings are held alternate months to discuss matters of common concern, and a modest Environmental Improvements budget is available to spend on projects that benefit the community. A newsletter is published periodically.

(Information supplied by Cathie French)

Ham Horticultural Society

Originally *Ham Cottagers Garden Society*, which was formed in the nineteenth century and revived nearly 50 years ago under its present name, this society is governed by a committee made up of members. Four Shows are held each year, Spring, Rose Show, Summer and Autumn; at these members can enter their garden produce in various categories; certificates and trophies are awarded after judging by an outside expert. There are also classes at the Shows for flower arranging and photography. The hut, off Lock Road, near the Ham Christian Centre, is owned by the Society, on land leased from Richmond Council. Each Sunday morning, members are able to buy a wide variety of aids to gardening; it also houses their stock of folding tables that are also borrowed for a number of local occasions, including Ham Fair (see pp.77–8).   (Information supplied by Denis Willis)

Petersham Horticultural Society

The Petersham Horticultural Society holds its annual Flower Show and Fete in the village hall, Petersham. The year 2000 sees their 94th Show. The Flower show takes a traditional village form and has classes for vegetables, flowers and fruit, together with home produce and art. There is a strong emphasis on children's work. There are also sideshows including children's games, Punch & Judy and raffle. The Society is run by an elected committee.

(Information supplied by Jim Kimbell)

Citizens' Advice Bureau, Ashburnham Road
This is an offshoot of the Richmond *CAB*, and is open on two mornings a week. Advice on legal and other personal problems is provided by trained volunteers.

The British Trust for Conservation Volunteers
The Trust, a charity that operates nationwide, has been active in several directions in our area over the past year or two. Sensory trails have been erected in the wooded part of the Common (see p.97) for the partially-sighted, clearance and dredging work done on Ham Pond, clearance and thinning-out on Ham Lands (see pp.88–90), willow planting and path making in Petersham Lodge Wood, work on the towpath, and on the Great Avenue to Ham House, where much work will be done in the year ahead.   L C

The Mary May Clarke Trust, 343 Petersham Road
The Trust provides crises care for the elderly on a temporary basis, particularly on discharge from hospital if help provided by Social Services is not adequate. Its resources are limited, but can provide some equipment for a limited time only, and will do all it can to meet particular needs.

The Fair Trials Abroad Trust, Bench House, Ham Street
Founded by way of an article in the *Independent*, its work includes legal representation and research into major defects in criminal justice systems worldwide. Surprisingly, over 80% of cases handled so far come from within the European Union. It has recently become a registered charity.

Ham Youth Club, Ham Hall
There is a dearth of activities for young people in Ham, so the Youth Club takes an essential place in the life of the Ward. It caters for youngsters from 8–23 years at various times in the week, under the leadership of Carol Manners. Games and activities are organised, including outside visits to museums and other places of interest in the London area. Other related activities are a club for young mothers, and training for the Duke of Edinburgh's Award Scheme in co-operation with Grey Court (see p.56).

Petersham United Charities
Grants from this charity are made for needy people in Petersham only, to cover such things as furniture, bedding, clothing, food, fuel, heating and educational purposes such as tools and books.

The wildlife of Ham

Editorial note: Of all the open spaces of Ham and Petersham, Ham Lands is of special significance, not only because of its turbulent history (see pp.116–17) but because of the richness and variety of its flora and fauna, which has become established or survived despite various kinds of human intervention. The survey of local wildlife concentrates, therefore, on this area. It has been prepared by a group of local people who have a wide knowledge of, and deep concern for, environmental issues, with John Hatto as co-ordinator. Other members of the group are Dr Paul Bartlett, Alison Fure, Dr Mary Foxworthy, Charles Henn, Freda & Geoff Hyde and Mary Parrilla; a few editorial interpolations have been made in this section, but any other substantial contribution has been individually acknowledged.

The survey made by the London Wildlife Trust [26] although now out of date (some species having disappeared, or appeared for the first time), is well worth studying. Much of the wildlife will have migrated from adjoining green spaces, and will still be found there.   L C

Ham Lands

The area we know and love as Ham Lands is of immense importance not only to local people but also to the whole of Greater London. It is a substantial area in itself, and an integral and complementary part of a wider system of local 'green' areas which is becoming relatively more valuable all the time, since the continuing growth of roads, building and agriculture causes increasing fragmentation and isolation. With their proximity to the River Thames, Home Park, Bushy Park, the Common and Richmond Park, the Lands form part of an invaluable 'green corridor' for wild life. In addition, Ham Lands has great visual and recreational value and always makes a pleasant and interesting walk, being especially attractive to dog-walkers, blackberry-pickers and natural history groups (see pp.76–7).

The wild life of Ham Lands has been evolving slowly and continuously since extraction from the gravel pits (see p.27) ceased in the 1950s. The substances used for infilling are important. Local Council sources have stated that rubble from the Chertsey Road extension was used, together with material from bomb site clearances. Possibly some chalk motorway tippings were included. Whatever the source of the infill, there is clearly a marked calcareous element to the flora of the Lands, evidenced by the presence of clematis, ploughman's spikenard, dropwort, orchids and other plants, all of which are lime-loving.

Possibly some of the alkalinity is due to the adjoining River Thames, that has a pH of about 7·0 which, although strictly speaking neutral, is very much towards the alkaline end of the spectrum in terms of plant preferences. This is in marked contrast to the other local 'green' areas such as Richmond Park, Bushy Park and Home Park, all of which have a more acid substrate: hence the importance of the Lands in increasing the range of species which can thrive in our Borough. Because the plants can grow here, many other species such as birds, butterflies and other insects, which depend on the plants, are attracted to the area.

The vegetation of the Lands is gradually evolving along the classical lines of plant succession towards eventual climax deciduous woodland. Coarse grasses, Japanese knotweed and hawthorn scrub increase all the time, and threaten to shade out and overwhelm the small, short-grassland species. This process poses problems in management (see pp.92–3), since if nothing were done there would be loss of species and less biodiversity. Hence the emphasis of management should be to maintain some areas of short grassland by an annual autumn mowing, after seed dispersal, with removal of the mowings to keep the nutrient levels low, so as to discourage the growth of coarse grasses. This is currently being done by the Council's Nature Conservation Department. Other areas could be left with different levels of vegetation to encourage a wider variety of species with different requirements. Some invasive species such as Japanese knotweed and sycamore should be removed where possible, and the hawthorn scrub, though valuable in moderation, should not be allowed to dominate.

Because, as mentioned above, the relative alkalinity of the Lands soils favours the growth of a much wider range of plant species than the more acid areas nearby, there is a long, varied and distinguished list of about 250 species of flowering plants which have been recorded there [26]. A number of these are rare, not only in the London area, but nationally as well, e.g. meadow and fingered saxifrages, grass vetchling and yellow vetchling, bee, spotted and pyramidal orchids, autumn squill, dropwort, dittander, moth mullein, maiden pink and Nottingham catchfly. Some of these appear to have been lost, but if their ecological requirements were maintained they could be found again, or could return.

Many other creatures are dependent on the plants for food, cover and nest-building, as discussed below.

Lovers of the Lands look forward to the new millennium with hope, encouragement and some confidence that with the current greater interest in, and understanding of, wild life, and a wider appreciation of the need to preserve our native species, the Lands will be safe as a nature reserve and preserved for posterity as a local treasure comparable to the others in our favoured borough.   Paul Bartlett

Birds of Ham Lands

Anyone using binoculars on the Lands is likely to be asked by a fellow-walker 'have you seen the parakeets?'. Yes, you almost certainly have, as they zoom about, advertising their presence by their cheerful squawking. They have increased rapidly in the area since a record of January 1992 noted a maximum of thirteen, and they do much damage to trees as well as crowding out other hole-nesting birds. They *are* beautiful birds, but so are the magpies and wood-pigeons which dominate the scene in the Lands in autumn and winter. How often do we really look at a magpie as we dismiss them for their prevalence and bad reputation as predators of smaller birds?

Apart from the parakeets, what is there that is interesting in autumn and winter? On the water (see pp.35–8, 74) there are gulls of several species and differing maturity, cormorants, herons and Canada geese (like the parakeets, these are 'aliens', as their name suggests), occasional mute swans, great crested grebes (less easy to identify in their winter plumage), little grebes in sheltered place and a variety of ducks. More ducks, of a wider range of species, appear as the weather gets worse and ponds and lakes freeze over. There will be coots and moorhens, and for the lucky careful observer there may be a kingfisher (see p.80). Pied wagtails are likely (they have a winter roost in the area and their call sounds like 'Chiswick') but grey wagtails are now rare.

In the more wooded areas there will be tits of three species; finches (including the scarcer, rather shy, bullfinch and in some winters parties of siskins or redpolls); jays — augmented in winter by migrants from the Continent; great spotted woodpeckers — with possibly lesser spotted; and treecreepers. Robins and wrens sing through the winter, and dunnocks flit about between the bushes. Tawny and little owls are resident but difficult to see. The former often move out onto built-up areas where they can be heard on winter nights.

In the more open, grassy areas, besides the magpies and crows, pigeons (both wood and the feral or 'London' ones) will be feeding on the ground, often joined by stock doves; and so will green woodpeckers and thrushes. Resident blackbirds, song- and mistle-thrushes will be joined by flocks of redwings and fieldfares from the north. These also feed on the berries which are a feature of the area. Some stay for the winter, others feast on the haw-thorns and move on. In any season a kestrel may be hovering overhead (far fewer of these than there used to be) or perched watchfully on a branch; a sparrowhawk may drift across.

Spring. When does it start? Song- and mistle-thrushes can be singing before Christmas and woodpeckers may be drumming in January, but, in the opinion of the writer, spring starts with the arrival of the first migrant chiff-chaffs in March. These are soon followed by willow and garden warblers, blackcaps, whitethroats and one or two lesser whitethroats. Overhead will be house martins, and a few swallows passing by. Later, swifts arrive, and on the Young Mariners' there will be common terns and perhaps a wader or two.

This is the time when the Lands really come alive. There is song everywhere as birds start setting up their territories. All this continues well into the summer, though song decreases as birds are busy feeding their young in the nest. This is a time when it is important not to disturb nesting birds, and dogs should kept well under control. Soon the young will be flying, and juveniles of unexpected species may be seen (e.g. the reed buntings in 1999). All too soon an absence of swifts will be noticed as the migration back south gets under way, and by the end of August the Lands seem comparatively empty of birds.

This is the regular cycle of bird life on Ham Lands, but in spring and autumn the lucky observer may come across a 'passage bird'. There is a long list of these birds which drop in for a while on their way elsewhere — hobby, redstarts, whinchat, sedge and reed warblers, wood warbler, spotted fly-catcher, brambling, nightingale (a singing male delighted walkers on Riverside Drive for two weeks in 1989, but, alas, failed to attract a mate), and various waders on the margins of the river and Young Mariners' or flying over. The nightingale was once a regular visitor to Ham Common (see p.99).

What changes have there been in the last ten years? There are certainly fewer swifts and house-martins. A large colony of swifts on Beaufort Court flats has all but disappeared since 1995, though a new colony is growing near the top of Ashburnham Road. A small colony of house-martins on St Thomas Aquinas Church had disappeared by 1997. There have been no skylarks or meadow-pipits for some time, grey wagtails and willow warblers seem to be down in numbers, as do starlings and house-sparrows, though the last two species are subject to a general decrease. There used to be stonechats (not recorded since January 1993) and occasional partridges or pheasants. Song-thrushes are endangered nationally, but seem to thrive on the Lands, and blackcaps and whitethroats are doing well also. But why these alterations? National trends play their part, as indicated above, as does management (especially the mowing regimes); but in the case of migrants, conditions in their wintering grounds and on the migration routes (e.g. the Sahara) have also to be taken into account.   Mary Parrilla

The Fauna of Ham and Petersham

Mammals include the Fox, Grey Squirrel, Hedgehog, Field Mouse, Weasel, Badger, Wood Mouse, Bank and Field Vole, Water Vole, Brown Rat, Common & Water Shrews and Bats in warmer weather. This stretch of Richmond's Riverside is one of the best areas in London in terms of the numbers and species diversity of feeding bats. The most commonly reported are pipistrelles, seroting, noctules and Daubenton's bats and some sightings of Leisler's, and a brown long-eared bat has been reported in the general area. Several bat walks have been held in the area, identifying various species by sonic detector.

Amphibians and Reptiles include, in warmer weather, Common Frog, Common Toad, Slow Worm (sighted again in 1998) and Grass Snake. There is also a recent unconfirmed report of an adder bite on adjoining lands.

From the Lands and other open spaces, several species have invaded gardens and local streets. At one time grey squirrels were seen only in the local wooded areas, but now they are everywhere, and nest in isolated trees. The fox has become well urbanised, and can be seen near houses in daylight. Even the badgers will come hunting for night-time food among the houses; some people leave food and water for them regularly. Apart from its place in nature, the badger, as a protected species, has an important effect on planning applications. However, badgers can also cause considerable damage to fruit and vegetables whilst searching for worms; there is a useful publication on this topic [30].

Invertebrates

These include 24 varieties of spider in one small sample area, the only such sampling carried out. The result of a more regular survey showed 15 varieties of butterfly, including Speckled Wood, Meadow Brown, Red Admiral, Painted Lady, Small Tortoiseshell, Peacock, Comma, Orange Tip and several varieties of Skippers and Blues. The moths of the area have not been listed, but cinnabar moths, their striped caterpillars feeding on the groundsel, are seen most years, as are burnet and hawk moths. 19 varieties of dragonfly have been seen in the Ham and Petersham area. On warm moist summer evenings swarms of insects can be seen rising like clouds from some of the larger riverside trees. This no doubt explains the many bats (see p.91); across London, however, insect numbers appear to be falling, so these sights may soon be seen less frequently.

Management of Ham Lands

Management is the most misunderstood practice on the Lands and to some residents mowing is synonymous with vandalism, but like many things it is the time the mowing takes place that is important in controlling some plants and encouraging others, thus allowing invertebrates, birds and other animals to prosper. If we simply let things grow we should soon find ourselves in a very dank and dark wood where nothing would thrive. Local people can remember when the part of the Common between the main road and the Park was grassland (see pp.97–9)!

Obviously, insects and other invertebrates are a vital part in the food chain and attract many animals including humans by their colour and beauty. Invertebrates often need different habitats at their different life stages of egg, larva and adult. So management must also aim to maintain appropriate habitats for all of these. Larger forms of wildlife also need conservation, particularly where vigorous forms or those better able to benefit from the actions of man may be upsetting the usual balance between predator and prey. Current reasons for management in the Lands also include flood control, safety, aesthetics, site accessibility as well the the conservation already discussed. In urban situations the primary aim of many open space managers is to maximise leisure and amenity interests. As already stated it is the time and frequency of the mowing that makes the difference, so watch for changes in mowing patterns, and don't be afraid to ask, because these changes may not be intended. Mowing at the wrong time may cause far more damage than missing out that particular mowing cycle.

Small mammal trapping in 1998

In October 1998 a small-scale study in three different habitats was undertaken on the Lands by staff and students from Roehampton Institute. These studies are widely used and involve the use of traps, provided with food and bedding, from which the animals are released, unharmed, after a few hours. The work was undertaken by licensed trappers; a total of 52 animals was caught — 50 wood mice and two bank voles. Five of the mice were recaptures, previously caught and marked. Such studies, confirmed by other observations, are used to indicate the mice population. Although only a small sample, this study suggested the area has a good number of small mammals. One area, the water meadow, contributed most of the captures and as it is regularly patrolled by owl and kestrels this appears to confirm the very high figures obtained for that part of the site.

Dangers to the Lands

(a) Rubbish dumping. This is a perennial problem, changing only in scale and material deposited, which can range from garden rubbish (both amateur and professional) to builder's rubble and cars. Local people should not hesitate to report observed instances, taking vehicle licence plate numbers, or looking for other incriminating evidence.

(b) Misuse by horses or cyclists. Neither is allowed on the Lands unless on a designated path. The dilemma is that winter flooding can cause hazardous conditions, and in case of accidents, the Council may be liable.

(c) Removal of plants. Removal of any wild flower or plant from a protected site such as the Lands is prohibited under the 1981 Countryside and Wildlife Act. The removal of fruit and seeds often deprives wildlife of vital winter food. Even teasels collected as decorations removes an important food source for goldfinches.

(d) 'Informal' residents. The record-holder for this activity scored about three years, but a close second is about to have his first anniversary. Earlier this year a larger community was broken up by the police burning their well-constructed 'lodge' of dead elms. Occasionally in the past caravans have been driven onto the Lands, though the deep ditch adjoining the road has helped to prevent this nuisance.

Other open land in Ham and Petersham

Ham and Petersham is fortunate to have so much open land locally; this has led to criticism of our conservation battles in the past, but such criticism tends to ignore the fact that the greater part of it is a Royal Park. A study of the Borough *Local wildlife sites map* in conjunction with the section on the Ward boundaries (see pp.33-5) will show the extent of open land in our Ward in comparison with other parts of the Borough.

The Gate House Garden
This is at the corner of Ham Common and Upper Ham Road, and was created from a site that for years was an eyesore and cause of complaint.

Through the initiative of Alys and Edward Brown, and the formation of the Ham Amenities Group (see p.81), it was possible to institute an investigation into the ownership of the land, eventually traced to the GLC who ultimately agreed to sell to the Group, after the site had been offered on the open market. About two thirds of the cost of purchase and of installing a water supply was donated by members, and the balance paid from Group funds. In 1983 work was completed; since then maintenance costs have been met by the Group and labour provided by its volunteers. There are seats for passers-by to relax in, and litter bins that are cleared regularly by the

Council. In 1995, through the further initiative of David Ripper, a former Group chairman, funds for a complete reconstruction of the Garden were obtain from the Borough's recycling revenues (see p.41).   L C

Richmond Park

The Park has an area of 955 hectares; its north-eastern border is only 13km from St Paul's Cathedral. An estimated three to four million visitors come each year, with large numbers visiting the Isabella Plantation at azalea time.

The Park forms the largest area of acidic grassland in Greater London, with a mosaic of other habitats. As recently as 1992 it was designated a Site of Special Scientific Interest, mainly because of its wealth of over 200 species of beetles, including many rarities. These are encouraged by a policy of not removing felled or fallen trees, thus creating ideal habitats for these creatures. English Nature has now suggested that the Park become a National Nature Reserve in recognition of the number and variety of the ancient trees.

The Park is the highest point in the Borough. Over two-thirds is covered by large open areas of grassland and bracken. There are, however, some serious concerns over the effect on birds and mammals (especially the deer) of unleashed dogs and litter. The place of the car is being hotly debated currently (see p.117).

There is no shortage of books describing the Park [5, 31, 33] and an official guide is also available [32]. Its origins, as they affect Ham and Petersham, and a Richmond brewer's successful fight to preserve public access are set out on pp.6-7. The Park is controlled by the Royal Parks Agency, whose decisions can only be overruled by Parliament, not by the Councils who border on the Park. Access is by road during daylight hours from 7am or 7.30am except when the annual cull of deer takes places. Pedestrians can enter by their own gates at any time of day or night. Only two of the major buildings in the Park are in our Ward: Pembroke Lodge and Thatched House Lodge. The former is a popular excursion for refreshments and strolls through the extensive gardens, and was formerly the home of the Russell family. At one time (see p.114) public access was in danger, apart from a proposed new restaurant at the extreme edge of the site. The views from the terrace and from other parts of the grounds are extensive. Thatched House Lodge is the home of Princess Alexandra and the Hon. Angus Ogilvy.

The control of the Park is in the hands of a police force separate from the Metropolitan Police; it has a mounted section and four-wheel drive vehicles to give access to all parts of its area. The Park has its own gardeners and staff

THE POND, HAM COMMON

PLANT 99

to manage the herd of 700 red and fallow deer, which give so much pleasure to visitors. Most of its car parks fall within our Ward: at Pembroke Lodge, Kingston Gate, Pen Ponds, Broomfield Hill Wood and Robin Hood Gate; there is also a smaller one for disabled badge holders on the edge of the Isabella Plantation. The direct access to this is by way of Ham Gate, which is under threat of closure (see p.117) if the more extreme traffic control measures suggested are put into effect.

The Park is a haven for wildlife, including fox, badger and many rabbits. Pen Ponds attracts many water birds, either passing through or nesting. Several enclosed areas encourage the shyer birds to take up residence; the variety of habitats available house a wide range of species.

Ham Common

This has an important part in the history of Ham (see pp.7 and below). It lies on River Terrace Gravels that give rise to a well-drained, slightly acidic soil. To the east of the main road the acid grassland has been largely replaced by a birch and oak wood, though in living memory cattle were seen to graze there. Many of the birch trees provide standing dead wood that is a valuable habitat for invertebrates. The open area to the east of the main road (see below) has Ham pond, where among the resident ducks, the occasional swan, the over-prevalent Canada geese and the visiting gulls a heron can be seen frequently perching on the 'no fishing' sign. Much has changed with the growth of the trees, and the rabbits that could be seen 65 years ago are no longer in evidence.

An historian views the Common

Calmly magnificent then will we turn   (Extract from the poem
The where the silver Thames first rural grows   *Summer* written in 1727 by
There let the feasted eye unwearied stray;   James Thomson
Luxurious, there, rove through the pendant woods (1700–1748)
That nodding hang o'er Harrington's retreat,
And stooping thence to Ham's embowering walks . . .

Sadly Ham's 'embowering walks' are now but a shadow of their former glory. Reminiscing on my life at Ham from the early 1930s, I recall what a joy it was to play under the Walk trees which had been planted to provide a walk, or avenue of trees, diagonally west across the Common to Lord Dysart's seat at Ham House. Age and Dutch Elm Disease took its toll. Only just discernible is footpath No.108 listed on the Definitive Map of Rights of Way running from the Richmond/Kingston road in a north-westerly direction to the road at the north side of the Common opposite the house called Jude Gate, once well-trodden by generations of village schoolchildren when being marched 'crocodile' fashion from their school (see p.19) to attend services at their Parish Church of St Andrew (see pp.50–1).

Cows grazed on the Common until 1933. Much in demand was Mr Harry T Adams of Ham Garage, Upper Ham Road, now St Andrew's House (see p.105), who apart from repairing motor, radio and electrical appliances, re-charged villagers' wireless accumulators. In 1937 the first shops on Ham Parade were built (see p.25). Large properties, some dating from the seventeenth and eighteenth centuries, are grouped around the triangular part of the Common, and the village pond, with its abundance of waterfowl completed a picture of affluence and tranquillity.

Apart from the natural spread of trees, special plantings were made to celebrate Coronations. An oak given by Mr Brawn commemorated Edward VII, a cedar marked that of George V, and in 1935 another tree commemorated the Silver Jubilee of the same King. The plantings of 1911 and 1935 can still be seen at the corner of Church Road, protected by railings. Up to 1935 Ham staged its own celebrations for national events , but the amalgamation with Richmond and Kingston made large-scale efforts impossible. The Jubilee festivities were held in the Old Deer Park, but Ham has the permanent reminder of this royal landmark.

Tree planting on the Common has continued, assisted by local schoolchildren and Scouts. In 1999 bluebells were planted near Ham Gate Avenue by local children, in unkind weather.

There are several lost landmarks of Ham Common. A First World War cannon, on the south side, viewable from the main road, gave pleasure to children, but was taken away for scrap metal in 1939, together with the railings of large local houses. A Common-keeper's hut could also be seen on that side and initially housed a small fire-engine to deal with the blazes that affected what was open land. A mound and sandpit near footpath 108, that covered the remains of General Eden's favourite charger (he lived in a cottage near Hardwicke House in the early nineteenth century) was levelled in the early 1950s. The General wished to see the village children play.

In September 1939, two T-shaped trench shelters were constructed in Ham School playground, one in Ham Street and another on the Common itself, close by footpath No.108 (see above), at a right angle to the main road.

On 13 September 1940, after an air raid, a large number of evacuees arrived from Stepney. They occupied the School shelters until billets were found for them that evening. Although some ate their meals with the host families, most had their mid-day meal at the British Kitchen run by the Women's Voluntary Service in South Lodge , a venue also used for First Aid and Home Nursing classes run by the British Red Cross Society. ARP (Air Raid Precautions) posts were set up in the garage and stable buildings at Ormeley Lodge and along Petersham Road by the site of the old post office in Petersham village. Ham's bird population suffered too, most notably the disappearance of the nightingale from the wooded part of the Common in the early 1940s, disturbed by the constant noise from tanks travelling along Park Road (now Ham Gate Avenue).

A different picture emerges in the 1950s. New developments at Parkleys, Bishop's Close (built on a site once locally referred to as 'Friars' Plot'), and Martingale's Close did not detract from the appearance of the Common. In Ham Gate Avenue, no new building took place, although Park Gate House was enlarged from 1983 onwards.

In 1987 a memorable event occurred when the hurricane of Friday 16 October damaged many of the Common's deciduous trees, including some willows around the Pond. Life changed little around the Common during the 1990s, except for increased traffic congestion and parked cars. A small development was built in the grounds of Latchmere House (see p.48), and the architect Julian Bicknell's imposing mansion, Forbes House, built between 1995 and 1999, will undoubtedly evoke admiration from many residents and visitors. This was on the site of the original Forbes House, two joined Georgian houses pulled down in 1935 and a later property, of the same name, designed that year by the architect Oswald Milne, itself demolished in 1992–3. Silvia Greenwood

Seats by the Pond

Close to St Thomas Aquinas church (see p.54) there is a seat dedicated to the memory of Mary and Richard Cave, from which the pond can be seen. Around the pond eight other seats are dedicated as follows (clockwise):
1. Harry Thomas Brown
2. Robert and Alys Brown, and Edward Brown
3. Richard Patterson
4. Given by the Ham and Petersham Ratepayers' and Residents' Association, 1987
5. Peggy Maclennan 1997 (given by the Ham Amenities Group)
6. As No.4
7. ? Doggett (lettering partly vandalised)
8. Given by the Ham Amenities Group 1985

Petersham Common

Covered by the 1902 Act (see p.23) and controlled by Conservators, this lies on London Clay, but its steep slope means it is well drained. At the top of the slope are many fine oaks, but conditions lower down favour hawthorn, hazel and field maple. The area is good for butterflies. An oak Regeneration Programme is in process, including selective felling and planting.

The Conservators control the maintenance and improvement of the Common, aided by a yearly budget from Richmond Council, who have two representatives on this body. Local residents are appointed to it, including two nominated by St Peter's Church (see p.49).

Petersham Meadows

Established and protected by Act of Parliament in 1902 (see pp.23–24) this piece of land, between the river and the main road, is the only surviving link with our Ward's agricultural past. It cannot be overrun by housing, but has been subject to planning proposals for buildings to extend the activities of Petersham Farm. Nonetheless, it remains green and open, still populated by cows and with a footpath across that entices many walkers, even if they must avoid pools of river water at times of high tides and other hazards consequent on grazing cows.

The planning history of the farm can be read in [15]. In recent years the cows have been kept as beef cattle, not as a milking herd, and with the current crisis of the farming industry generally there was a danger that their owners would not be able to feed them during the winter. In 1997, on the initiative of local resident Chris Brasher, a public meeting was held in the Village Hall to put pressure on Richmond Council to ensure that grazing continued for the major part of the year. The budget for open spaces in the Borough was not sufficient to cover the feeding of cattle, so private contributions were made to cover this, to keep fences in repair and to cover legal costs. A new lease was eventually negotiated with the farm owners that allowed 22 acres of the Meadows to revert to the Council in exchange for permission for horses to graze on two small fields forming part of the Meadows. Since then the Petersham Trust, a registered charity, has been established, with representatives from the Ham and Petersham Association, the Council and the Richmond Society, who have a natural interest in the View from Richmond Hill. The current position is that certain difficulties have arisen over the question of the farm lease, and until these are resolved, the Trust's own lease cannot be finalised. It is hoped that eventually the Meadows will be managed by the National Trust, in conjunction with that of Ham House and its surrounds. In the meantime, generous donations to the Trust continue to arrive. (Information extracted from material circulated by the Ham and Petersham Association; the full text has been deposited in the Local Studies Room)

Shopping in Ham and Petersham

The greater availability of personal transport enables many people to travel farther and to carry heavier loads when shopping for everyday necessities; this has helped to bring about the advance of Supermarket and Hypermarket shopping. Nearly all the basic consumables, from food and drink, domestic and some pharmaceutical goods, casual and every-day clothes may be available under one roof and it is no longer essential to shop separately for materials, books, tools and plants for the ever popular DIY activities of home maintenance, decorating and gardening as there are also Supermarkets for these. Household furniture and linens are found either here or in large department stores. The modern Shopping Mall is the place for the latest fashions and luxury goods, where customers can relax, take refreshment and window-shop.

Ham and Petersham at the beginning of 2000 has neither large Supermarket nor Shopping Mall. The largest group of shops is along the Upper Ham Road, both sides known as Ham Parade. This in itself is a reminder that Ham retains much that was valued in the past — many a Parade has disappeared in the process described above, and we are fortunate that nearly all our basic needs and some frivolities can be supplied by our local shops.

On the Parade there are two each of hairdressers, bakers, dry-cleaners (one of which repairs shoes and cuts keys, the other repairs clothes), newsagents (both of which sell sweets, cigarettes, greetings cards and stationery and have a photocopier; in one there is also a Post Office Counter). There are two off-licences (one is within a small Supermarket) and two hardware shops which between them can supply everything one might need to repair or decorate the home, or shoes, or the garden, plus pet food and bedding, mousetraps and other pest control products, kindling and Coalite for the hearth.

There is a large pharmacy, a well-stocked greengrocery and a butcher's shop, two beauty parlours and another just off the Parade, nearer to Ham Common, for grooming dogs. Three banks still maintained sub-branches at the end of 1999, though one is about to close as this book goes to press, and we have no less than three estate agents. Less basic needs are served by a high quality delicatessen, an antiques shop, a stationers which also sells a few novelties, a ladies' fashion shop, travel agent, launderette, betting shop, mobile phone supplier and one specialising in pine furniture. Eating out is catered for by four establishments: Chinese, Indian, Italian and a café-restaurant, the first two of which also have take-away facilities. Near the

Common also are a florist and a small shop selling gifts and novelties.

The small Supermarket mentioned above is about the size of two or three shops and carries a wide stock of fresh, preserved, cold or frozen foods plus cigarettes and sweets and the off-licence, fax and photocopying facilities. Like many of the shops in Ham it is a family business.

The southern part of Ham Street was once the main shopping street of the village, containing evidence and memories of past business. On one house a key is engraved, suggesting that the bootmaker who once inhabited it also cut keys, a bay window in a small house replaced the front of a confectioner's shop, and many remember the shop owned by the London Co-operative Society until 1979, now a large house. On the site of two former shops, themselves replacing an ancient Public House (see p.65) is a family business, still called Ham Stores, which supplies a very wide range of foods, canned, refrigerated or frozen, plus many other domestic requirements, including fresh supplies of milk and bread each day; it stocks newspapers and is also an off-licence. It opens every day of the year for twelve hours a day, except for Christmas Day, when it closes early. In the days before extended opening hours and Sunday opening became common, it was the refuge for the improvident, the late and for those with unexpected visitors, but now suffers fiercer competition.

In Back Lane, another part of old Ham, is a small parade of shops with an award-winning Post Office (also selling newspapers, sweets and cigarettes) another pharmacy with photocopying and a hairdressers. Near to the footway called The Bench is yet another hairdressers. In Ham Street/Ashburnham Road opposite the Library (see p.75) is an L-shaped block of shops built in 1958–9 (see p.27). Here, opposite Grey Court School (see pp.55–6) can be found a Chinese take-away that is also the local fish-and-chips shop (seating available inside), a dry-cleaner, yet another hairdresser and a shop specialising in decorative coloured transfers. On the corner is a pizza and pasta take-away (at one time this was an Optometrists), and shops selling carpets and flooring, an off-licence, an Indian takeaway and a small Supermarket that sells food, cigarettes, sweets and newspapers and has a photocopier. Several service establishments can be found here, one for repairing television sets, radios, hi-fi equipment and computers and one that is a motorcycle hire and training centre. Several small shops have opened and closed in this block over recent years, with the premises remaining unoccupied for months at a time (there are two vacant at the moment), but there are one or two notable exceptions that have earned their place by serving the local community well.

Near St Richard's Church (see p.53) a parade of shops was built at the time the Wates development took place (see p.27). The original intention was to erect another block at right angles to it, but when building was confined to one side of what was to be the spine road for the development, flats for private sale were put up instead. Here can be found a newsagent, Chinese takeaway, German bakery that has tables for coffee and cakes, pharmacy with photocopier and Fax facilities, video hire shop, butcher who sells greengroceries, flowers and seasonal plants, another off-licence and a supermarket, with extended hours that sells mainly food, but also newspapers.

Petersham now has no shops, but does boast a Garden Centre (see p.104) and farm shop; an unending supply of cut-price pots is available at what used to be the Forge Garage. One business remains at the Ham end of the main road, a long-established photographer near the Fox and Goose public house. There are other shopping opportunities at a parade of shops built in the mid-1930s as part of the large Tudor Estate that is part of Kingston, but is very near the border of our Ward. Here there is yet another hairdresser, a pharmacy, small food supermarket, greengrocer/florist, newsagent and well-stocked hardware store that also sells haberdashery. From Ham Cross can be seen the St George's industrial estate, which has retail counters for timber, electrical goods, paint, batteries and spare parts for cars, and a glazier. More extensive shopping facilities are in Kingston, which boasts a crowded Monday market and a good street market on most other days; Kingston is a shopping magnet for miles around. Richmond has a good, if smaller-scale, selection of shops and many restaurants.

What conclusions can be drawn from this mixture? It could be surmised, lightheartedly, that Ham and Petersham is full of exquisitely-coiffured ladies and gentlemen who enjoy food and wine, are quite adept at house maintenance and repairs, voracious readers of newspapers who communicate by means of modern technology, but may be subject to a degree of hypochondria!

The truth is deeper, however. The pattern of shopping must be very reminiscent of what it was over half a century ago, though on a less intensive scale, with a lively mixture of shops for essential goods expanding in line with the growth of the area, and developing with changes in present-day requirements. The increase in shopping by Internet may not have a catastrophic effect on local shopping, since, in any case, much of it will probably be directed at what would have been large Supermarket purchases. We can only hope that the demand for instant supply will be sufficient to keep our good friends in business. There is already some shopping from home, served by a mobile greengrocer, a mobile fishmonger and the familiar milkman, now freelance rather than an employee of a large dairy, who also delivers bread and groceries where required. One newsagent alone delivers newspapers and magazines daily to over 400 householders. Local take-aways will also deliver meals if required, as will pizza parlours.   C N

Lottery outlets

Ham is well supplied with National Lottery outlets. There are two in Ham Parade (see p.101), one in Back Lane (see p.102) and two in the parade of shops by St Richard's Church (see p.103). The only outlet in Ham Street (see p.102) closed when the newsagent there went out of business.

A visit to the barber

Since moving into Ham in the '60s, my memories of what it was like then have become somewhat dim, but one clear recollection I still have is that of taking my young sons to have their hair cut by the Ham Village Barber. The flower shop on the Common, now known as 'Pick of the Bunch' was then a newsagent and sweet shop, and by walking through this to the back you came upon the Barber's shop.

It wasn't necessary to make an appointment, so usually on arrival a short wait would be needed. This was never a boring time, more an informative one. The chit-chat there between Barber and client was nothing like the small talk of the modern unisex hairdresser; it was all about the local news and gossip. When the boys' turn arrived a bridge was put across the chair and their hair cuts would proceed one after the other. At the finish a big bag of sweets would appear for two eager hands to delve into. Then we left — two neat heads munching sweets and myself up to date with local news: the cost was 2/- (10p) each cut!   Jean Sandford

Petersham Nurseries

The Nurseries lie at the back of Petersham House, reached by an unmade lane by the side of St Peter's Church or on foot from River Lane. Founded after World War II, it has provided an accessible source of plants and garden accessories for many years, though recently there was a threat of the land being sold for the building of a single large private house.

Employment

Before the division of Ham in 1933 (see p.25), which took the local factory firmly into Kingston, Ham's largest local employer was the Leyland motor works, later Hawker Siddley Aviation and finally British Aerospace. Until this factory closed, it provided many jobs for local people particularly, and it was a tragedy that so many skilled men who lived near their place of work were forced to look elsewhere, or take different employment. Other centres of employment were farms (see pp.19–20) and gravel workings (see p.24).

Although there is now no obvious centre of large-scale employment, Ham and Petersham are not devoid of job opportunities; every shop, school, pub, medical practice or local authority service can give employment to local people. A few enterprises are active in the district, apart from those that are carried on from home, though they are mostly discreetly integrated into surrounding buildings.

Ham Parade has our only local solicitor, Dixon, Ward & Co, associated with the practice on Richmond Green, but operating quite independently. It occupies Sarah Morffew's old cottage [24], extended at the side. It also has Sanders, our local undertakers; their premises were formerly on the opposite side of the road, but the new building enabled them to open a Chapel of Rest and to operate independently from the Richmond branch. Near the corner of Dukes Avenue is the office of Harriscourt Industrial Holdings Ltd.

Ham Common has two professional offices, both in St Andrew's House, formerly the local garage, later a World War II 'shadow factory' until badly damaged by a wartime bomb. Riches Consulting offers a range of financial and business management consulting services both locally and internationally, including advice for companies wishing to trade in Azerbaijan or China. Discover the World act as consultants to several airlines on sales and marketing, with an office in America.

Lock Road houses Chase: 3C, a debt collection and tracing agency in the small building that was once Ham UDC offices, later a rent collection office.

Back Lane has COPROM, next door to the hairdresser's. This company obtains promotional products for businesses to give to clients, having most of their contacts in Central London.

Petersham Road had a builder who advertised his services on a board outside his house; now the sign advertises domestic engineering only.

Transport

Cycle Routes

Our Borough is committed to supporting cycling as part of a strategy for sustainable transport and a better environment, and is working together with other London boroughs in supporting and implementing the London Cycle Network. The Thames Cycle Route runs across Richmond Park to Ham

Gate, along Ham Gate Avenue and crosses the main road by the traffic lights
to the north side of the Common, continuing the whole length of Lock Road.
At the junction it turns right, then into Hardwicke Road, crosses Duke's
Avenue into Thamesgate Close, then to Teddington Lock, where it continues in both directions to Kingston or Richmond. Other cycle routes in
Ham are from Kingston via Richmond Road or Tudor Drive. The first
continues to the Common and takes the southern side to the great avenue
that leads to the back of Ham House, joining the River Path by the side of
the House and across to the ferry steps. The latter follows Dukes Avenue to
join the River Path to the Lock, or continues by the Thames Young Mariners' base and the side of the Walnut Tree allotments to Ham Street, where it
turns left to the River. The name 'Sustrans' appears from time to time in
literature concerning the cycle paths: an abbreviation for 'Sustainable
Transport'. There are cycle route maps available from both Richmond and
Kingston; they do not quite agree. A guide is also available from Richmond
Park, pointing out that off road cycling is not allowed, and showing the
authorised Tamsin Trail and the continuation of the Thames Cycle Route.

Proposals have been made for the footpath by the side of Ham Gate
Avenue to be widened and made a joint cycle and footpath. As it has always
been a walker's path, some conflict of interest is likely, especially with cycles
coming in both directions.   L C

Horses in Ham and Petersham

The number of horses and ponies kept in Ham and Petersham in 2000 may
well be higher than at any time during the previous century. The historic use
of horses can be seen on pp. 11–13; they are here now for pleasure only, but
few are stabled at home. There is a livery yard run by Kingston Riding
Centre at Petersham Farm, stabling some 15 or 20; they are lucky enough to
have access to grazing on the Farm. Ham House Stables (now separate from
the House) accommodates 12 horses for teaching and livery services. These are
trained for dressage, jumping and of course hacking. Manor Farm Stables,
situated on the old site of Petersham Manor Farm to the east of the polo
field, keeps both polo (see below) and livery horses ; in summer about 70
horses reside there. Richmond Park has both police and dray horses.

We are incredibly lucky to have extensive and beautiful riding tracks:
Ham Fields, The Copse and along the Great Avenue to Ham House. At
Ham Common an unsurfaced track leads to Richmond Park, across and
around which other tracks can be found. Intrepid riders can even cross the A3
and go to Wimbledon Common. In Ham Common, among the trees, there is
a small clearing where horses can be worked.

The Polo Club, one of the oldest in Great Britain, was first established in 1926, situated near the Common. It moved to its present site, adjacent to Ham House, in 1954. In 1996 the Club purchased the adjacent land and the original Equestrian Club premises near Ham Gate were sold. The ponies were moved to the yards next to the polo field. The Club is now a flourishing concern, where exciting games are played by skilled players at weekends throughout the summer, with free entry to spectators on foot. (Full text of this contribution by Minette Rice Edwards is in the Local Studies Room)

(Outside the area covered by this book is the Barnfield Riding Stables, where pupils from Strathmore School use their 'Riding for the Disables' facilities.)

Motoring in Ham and Petersham

Motoring in the area is both a blessing and a curse: the former when the individual is faced with an awkward journey, or a shortage of time for local needs, and the latter when progress through the narrow part of Petersham is made nearly impossible by the weight of traffic using the area as a through route, when roads are obstructed by double parking or removal vans parked for long periods, by accidents or broken-down vehicles. There seems to be no solution to the increase of traffic; parking problems could be eased by the use of garages that are either left empty overnight or filled with household effects, but a large number of dwellings have no provision for off-street parking, even a proportion of more modern ones such as the earlier flats and maisonettes on the Wates estate.

The local motorist is well served if a new car is not required. Used cars are sold in Duke's Avenue, MOT tests can be conducted next door or off Warners Lane (see p.22), behind the Water Gipsies public house (petrol and car wash facilities are also available here) or in the centre of Petersham, where the old forge used to be. Coming from Kingston on the A307, Ham has the last petrol filling station before the Chiswick roundabout, those in the centre of Richmond having closed down some years ago.

There are at present no parking meters in Ham and Petersham.

Bus services

Ham and Petersham is entirely dependent on buses for public transport; if radius lines are drawn around railway stations in the Borough it will seen how badly we are served by rail in comparison with other parts. A document exists in the Surrey Records Office showing a nineteenth century proposal to build a railway branch line from Norbiton to Ham; had this happened it would probably have accelerated the rate of house building, but Dr Beeching would surely have closed it down! No electric trams ran within the borough of Richmond; the 69 route ran from Twickenham, Teddington and Kingston to the old Ham border during peak hours, but once it made its last journey in June 1931 the bus reigned supreme.

In 1845 (see p.12) the first bus ran: there can be no doubt which route it took. 105 years later a new route was introduced. With the break-up of London Transport we are now served by four separate companies, though all are regulated by London Buses, and accept Freedom Passes (see below). The worst (or best) may be yet to come if ever deregulation arrives.   L C

Route 65. This is the traditional route along the A 307, which has survived two World Wars and the Petersham Hole (see p.31). It is now run by Armchair with double deck vehicles, now mostly somewhat ageing, in an orange and white livery, and provides a link to Kingston, Richmond, Brentford and Ealing. At one time it ran to Hook, Chessington and even beyond, but now has a shorter route.

Route 371. This route can be considered as our 'local' bus to Richmond and Kingston, serving Richmond Hill and North Kingston also. In contrast with the unvarying path of the 65, it was rerouted several times when it was the double-deck 71 route, first introduced exactly 50 years ago. At that time the Wates estate was hardly a gleam in the developer's eye, and it served mainly the inter-war part of Ham, coming across from North Kingston into Dukes Avenue, into Dysart Avenue, Lammas Road, then across into Broughton Avenue and along Lock Road to the Common, where it joined the 65 route into Richmond, using the lower road rather than the Hill. In 1968 the route was altered to take in the new Wates development; omitting Lammas Road it turned into Broughton Avenue, turned right into Ashburnham Road to Ham Street and via Sandy Lane to the main road. At one point a further rerouteing to take it along Riverside Drive was fought off by local opposition. Local pressure also gained a Sunday service, despite official forecasts that numbers would not justify this; of course the local people were right. Later it was taken away from the lower road to serve Richmond Hill, and since then its path has been more or less stable. When Westlink (now owned by London United) took the route over it was made a single-deck route and renumbered (the 71 still took the part of the route from Kingston to Chessington). The new frequency was nearly double that of the former 71, though traffic conditions at each end of its route make running to timetable very difficult. The red buses, already replaced once, and now including some low-loading vehicles, carry large slogans on the side, such as 'Going to St Peter's? You'll appreciate our Sunday Service' and even has a German slogan for the School.

HAMMERTON'S FERRY

PLANT 99

Once a day in each direction a double-deck service, run by Armchair, takes schoolchildren to and from Grey Court School; it does not accept ordinary passengers, who would probably avoid it in any case! There is considerable local affection for the route at its best (including the late evening ones which run until 12.40am from Richmond Station); the majority of passengers thank the drivers on their way out through the front exits.

Route 485. These little green buses, operated now by Telling's Golden Miller, run six times a day in each direction from Richmond to Ham via Kew, Mortlake, Barnes, Putney Common, Roehampton, Kingston Hospital and the back streets of North Kingston, taking 1 hour 20 minutes for the full journey. Alternate buses have facilities for taking wheelchairs. The route from Ham was originally the K6, that served passengers off the main Kingston routes, and was combined with service R61 that formed a link between hospitals. The passengers who use it regularly after shopping seem to know each other and the driver well; occasional users can feel that they have strayed onto a village bus by accident.

Buses for the disabled. Two 'Mobility Bus' routes serve Ham and Petersham: Nos. 938 and 964. They are designed to accommodate wheelchairs, and are run by Thorpe's Coaches, using minibuses in a yellow and red livery. 938 runs on Mondays only from Chessington to Richmond via Ham in the morning, returning late in the afternoon. 964 runs on Tuesday and Friday from Kew to Kingston via Ham in the morning, returning in the afternoon. As well as serving shopping centres, buses serve Ham House in the summer, and also Ham Day Centre (see p.44). Timetables can be obtained on request; at one time these were posted on bus stops, but have recently disappeared. We are also served by the 'Dial-a-bus' minibuses.

Countdown

This is a new system of bus information, mounted on bus shelters and giving electronic advice of when the next bus is due. It claims to have been installed throughout Kingston; the map in its informative brochure shows our routes south of the Sandy Lane junction as being covered, but installation is patchy. At the turn of the year there were but four stops served on the 65 route, and the position on the 371 route is even sparser, with only one installation for Richmond-bound buses opposite Ham Library, and none at all for the whole of the route in the opposite direction. It is to be hoped that the system will be extended eventually, as it would be of enormous help to those worried by the erratic nature of our local service (see p.108). It can only be installed where a bus shelter is available, which is impossible on the narrow pavements of most of Petersham.

The Freedom Pass

Throughout the Greater London Area these passes are issued bi-annually to pensioners, women at 60 and men at 65. When first issued they allowed free travel on buses and underground trains only, but later this privilege was extended to the overground railway system, though at a slightly later starting time. They are highly prized and well used, saving very many car journeys. Each costs our Borough about £300 per year; those who take this privilege without putting it to use are therefore rather wasting ratepayers' money. At some point in the future these could be withdrawn, but it would need a concerted effort by all London councils to achieve this; at the moment those of us who own them are safe until the year 2002.

River transport

The River Thames is full of passenger-carrying craft (see pp.35–3), but the only one that can be boarded in our Ward is the Ferry to Twickenham (see pp.14–15, 34–5). Although passenger steamers are held up at Teddington Lock, it is not possible to board them there, through the hardy may decide to 'jump ship' on a return journey without proper authority.

Aircraft

Strictly speaking, these should not come into this survey, yet their noise is always with us, particularly the overpowering noise of Concorde, which has ruined many an interesting conversation or radio feature. Ham and Petersham is less troubled by aircraft noise compared with Richmond and Kew, yet on fine days, aircraft taking off from Heathrow over our Ward do constitute a nuisance, which will be aggravated if the current proposals for building a fifth terminal are approved. Night flights are also liable to be extended at any time should our Government so decree, and current proposals for giant jets may cause further problems. Yet we are quite grateful for the proximity of Heathrow when we fly off on holiday and business, or meet visitors from overseas, and we have got to live with our present problems unless a radical solution is found.

The Postal Service

Ham and Petersham are remote from their sorting office. Originally this was at Richmond, but was later removed to Twickenham. The delivery service is quite reliable, and our postmen normally very helpful. If parcels cannot be delivered, or left in the safe custody of a neighbour, it is possible to collect them; an office near the Old Deer Park is open for them to be picked up. The bundled daily post is first delivered to 'pouch boxes', of which examples can be seen by the 'Fox and Duck' and in Kingfisher Drive, from which our local postmen can collect for delivery to individual houses. For outgoing mail, there is a sufficient supply of postboxes (including one Victorian example in the wall by St Andrew's Church), with four collections being made on Monday–Friday and two on Saturday. On Sunday there is a collection at 12.45 from that near the post office in Back Lane, and at 1pm from outside the post office in Ham Parade. One slight anomaly is that this postbox is still cleared by Kingston, in spite of boundary changes; this gives us the advantage of using it for quicker delivery to KT postcodes, but those for TW postcodes letters may best be placed in other boxes.

If Ham and Petersham has one major quarrel with the Post Office it is that our name has been abolished. The 'correct' (*sic*) postal address is Richmond only, which is incorrect geographically, and could lead to confusion, especially when estate agents ignore the proper location of houses they advertise. Any business using a mailing list based on postcodes will always omit Ham or Petersham; sometimes a request to use our proper village names will be complied with. Perhaps one of the future Millennium battles (see pp.114–17) could be to restore our names in the way that has been done for Hampton Wick: lack of use can lead to loss of identity (e.g. Hatch and many other examples).   L C

Newspapers and Freesheets

There are three local newspapers that are sold, and therefore read, and several 'freesheets', none of which seems to achieve a total distribution in our area. In addition, a glossy magazine whose prime purpose is to advertise houses for sale has recently appeared, though because its distribution area seems haphazard, many people are not aware of its existence.   L C

The Richmond and Twickenham Times
This was not our earliest local newspaper (see p.22) but it can be considered as the prime publication for our area. Owned by the Dimbleby family, it is the only one remaining in broadsheet form. It publishes at least two full pages of letters every Friday, of which Ham and Petersham people take full advantage to air local issues, though they very seldom write on less controversial subjects. It also publishes a generous selection of photographs of local events, and is quite responsive to calls for photographers and to press hand-

outs. It gives full arts coverage and a comprehensive listing of forthcoming local events. Its spelling and grammar are occasionally fallible, and it is sometimes guilty of writing headlines that have nothing to do with the matter beneath them. But if it disappeared, or was forced to resort to Internet publishing only, it would be sadly missed.

The Richmond Comet
This is published by the *Surrey Comet*, the oldest newspaper in our area (see p.22), and its masthead claims to be the 'best for' all areas in the borough (though it omits Ham and Petersham). None the less it does publish material regularly concerning our Ward, though its bias is towards Kingston borough, where its publishing offices are situated. It is a tabloid published each Friday, contains only a few letters, but has thorough coverage of the arts.

The Richmond Chronicle
This is a relative newcomer, claiming to be 'the number one paper for Ham' (Petersham is not mentioned in its masthead), published by the Middlesex County Press, a division of Southnews plc, at the same office as the *Informer* (see below). It is a lively tabloid, published on Thursday and priced to undercut other local papers. It has a reasonably full news coverage, publishes a page of letters, and covers all aspects of the arts but lacks the comprehensive listings of our senior local newspaper.

The Richmond and Twickenham Informer
Published by South News plc, (see above, but note that the discrepancy in spelling is that of the newspaper itself) in Teddington, this tabloid freesheet is part of a series of three newspapers covering Richmond, Kingston & Walton. Its masthead does not mention Ham or Petersham, though it is widely distributed here. Over half the content is advertisements, (including a large number of 'small ads.' and car adverts); it has a sketchy coverage of news, a handful of letters and covers only the more 'popular' arts news or reviews. It is also sold through newsagents at a price even lower than the *Chronicle*.

The Richmond Borough Guardian
This is another tabloid freesheet, published on Thursdays from North Cheam by Newsquest — a Gannett Company.It has a larger coverage of news than other local freesheets, whilst containing over 50% advertising. Given that it is published so far from Richmond, its local news coverage seems quite good, though the choice of 'Scene' for its arts section suggests that its interest in that area is less than comprehensive.

The Richmond Magazine

This is also a freesheet, published monthly, but of a special quality, though its distribution area in our Ward is difficult to understand. It can be obtained at the Richmond Tourist Information Office by those who do not receive copies through their letterboxes. It is a full colour publication in magazine format, printed on glossy paper; its main purpose is to advertise property at the middle and higher price ranges. It has a selection of articles of general or local interest, well presented if not always of great depth, and will publicise forthcoming local events. It is published by Sheengate Publishing Ltd from Chessington; it has certainly added a colourful dimension to local journalism.

Property News

At one time this freesheet was delivered through the letterbox, but now seems available only from local estate agents or by purchase. It is a tabloid devoted solely to property advertisements, and with no editorial content.

Battles in Ham and Petersham

Throughout their history, the people of Ham and Petersham have fought, not always successfully, to preserve their lands and their rights. In the English Civil War there was no battle recorded, though A Anderson records in his *History of Kingston* (1818) that a grand rendezvous of the victorious Parliamentary troops took place on Ham Common. The fight to preserve the independence of Ham has been mentioned already (p.25); Ham UDC increased the rates to cover the cost of this, and would have fought on a technicality beyond 1933 but for legal advice that they were unlikely to win. From the time of incorporation into Richmond a series of battles were fought over individual planning issues and much larger ones too, by the Ratepayers' and Residents' Association (see p.82). These are covered in *Life in Ham and Petersham*[15]; the booklet tells of the Petersham By-pass, proposed 9-storey flats on Ham Close, preservation of Ham Lands (see below), developments at the Ham Manor House site that would have encroached on the Great Avenue to Ham House, over-development at Petersham Manor Farm stables and Petersham Farm, and in 1987 an attempt by Kingston Council to take over a substantial part of Ham. In the same year proposals were made to sell Pembroke Lodge to a private buyer, thus depriving visitors of a notable refreshment site and the extensive view that went with it; this was fought off successfully, though the danger must still remain. Accounts of two actions, one a crusade by a local resident and one a community fight, appear below.

King Henry's Mound and the view of St Paul's

Not long after the completion of Wren's new St Paul's Cathedral in 1710, although the great Dome of St Peter's in Rome had been familiar to Englishmen on the Grand Tour for over 120 years, Wren's masterpiece was a welcome, though revolutionary, design for England. The decision to plant an avenue of trees, starting at the highest point in Richmond Park and aligned directly onto the new Cathedral 10 miles away must have caused immediate excited enthusiasm. From that point on St Paul's became framed in trees.

In the early nineteenth century, however, the sole purpose of the avenue's planting was nearly put at risk with the plan in 1823 to cover a large part of the high ground in the Park with the Sidmouth Plantation. Fortunately a long straight ride and pathway was landscaped through it, and the remarkable vista survived. It was during the tenure of Pembroke Lodge by the Prime Minister, Lord John Russell and his family in the second half of the nineteenth century that the essentials of the present landscaping at the Mound were probably carried out, leaving, eastward, a 'keyhole' in the great holly hedge in which St Paul's remained framed.

All this we can see today, but for nearly 40 years after the outbreak of the Second World War the view became obscured by the untended growth of the holly hedge, and in Sidmouth Wood itself. The increasing preponderance of high-rise buildings in London after the 1960s posed another threat to an historic view that had been almost entirely forgotten.

In the early months of 1976 a resident of Ham Common, James Batten, began to ponder on the purpose of the planting shown on Roque's eighteenth-century map of London. As a student he had visited Rome many times, and become accustomed to the visual interlinking of fine architecture by means of connecting vistas, including that of St Peter's and the 'keyhole vista' in the garden gates of the Knights of Malta on the Aventine Hill. The parallel was clear to him, and as soon as possible he went to King Henry's Mound, to find the holly hedge now totally dense. The following day he returned, but in endeavouring to fight his way through the hedge became caught up on some twisted, rusty metal that proved to be part of the original trellaced arbour. Stepping over this and parting the branches he saw the view to St Paul's.

Within a few days of this rediscovery, he heard that British Rail was well into preparing plans to redevelop Liverpool Street Station with a high rise building. Knowing that the station stood on the St Paul's axis, it was clear to him that the view of the Cathedral's dome and drum would then be against a vast rectangular glass box. An architect friend told him that there was already a group of concerned conservation bodies putting together a case against the development, and suggested they might welcome further arguments in support, albeit from ten miles away.

James Batten returned to the Mound and cleared some of the holly, then told the Park authorities of what he had discovered, though the battered, but once graceful arbour was taken away and somehow 'lost'. He then set to work in preparing his case, supported at the subsequent Inquiry by fine photographs taken from the Mound by the now alerted GLC planning department. The Public Inquiry began at the end of 1976 and ended the following February; the Inspector's report, (March 1979) which noted the importance of the 10-mile vista, resulted in a rejection of the British Rail application, yet it was not until 1992 that legal protection for 'the strategic view of St Paul's Cathedral from King Henry VIII's Mound and its viewing corridor' was finally given.

In the intervening years James Batten had to remain on the alert as more and more high developments were mooted on or near the vista line, not infrequently seeking interviews with major developers to call their attention to the effect their plans might have on the vista. He also tried at every opportunity to give a wider awareness worldwide of the importance of this preservation battle. The present appearance of the area around the Mound, with its explanatory display boards, is a tribute to all who fought the battle.   (Condensed: James Batten's full account has been placed in the Local Studies Room)

The fight for Ham Lands

When gravel workings were exhausted (see p.27) 93 acres became available for development. In 1959 and 1960 public meetings were called by the (then) HPRA (see p.82) to recommend that the whole of the lands should be reserved for public open space and playing fields; by 1963, however, building on the 60 acres by Wates was in progress, and by 1968 this large estate was completed. There still remained 33 acres, which were to be the subject of a long battle. An application by Wates to continue building was refused, but the subsequent re-organisation of government, with the creation of the enlarged borough of Richmond upon Thames and the Greater London Council brought pressure for social housing on 15 of the remaining acres. The first plan included four 5-storey blocks, two 7-storey blocks and one 8-storey block; a public meeting was held, and local opposition was supported by a number of prominent bodies. This scheme did not go forward, but in 1972 three Housing Associations put forward plans for building in a narrow strip between Beaufort Court and the Croft Way garage. The first Ham Lands Action Committee was formed, bringing together the HPRA, the Ham Riverside Residents' Association and all three local branches of the main political parties, under the chairmanship of the HRRA representative, to fight the proposals at Public Inquiry. The fight was lost in 1975; planning permission was given, but with a limited time period; by the time this expired the Housing Associations had not proceeded (probably due to the high cost of the land in question), but in 1979 the then Conservative Council gave permission for the Locksmeade Estate to be built. The Action Committee was reformed to fight any subsequent planning proposals for the remaining 10 acres, headed this time by David Williams, whose contribution to the first inquiry had excited admiration even from the opposing interests, but with the election of a Liberal Council, the unbuilt area was declared Metropolitan Open Land, thus protecting its future (see pp.88–91).

Current battles
These are amply reflected in reports and in the correspondence columns of the *Richmond and Twickenham Times*, our major local newspaper (see pp.112–13) and include (a) efforts to restore the historic view of Ham House from the Common by clearing away the encroaching undergrowth, (b) control on exercise of horses by Ham Polo Club (see p.107), (c) the rising tide of vandalism and graffiti, (d) traffic calming measures, and, as the book goes to press, proposed severe cut in Library hours (see p.76). The largest battle looming is concerning proposals that the roads of Richmond Park (see pp.95–6) shall be wholly or partly closed to cars. Experience during times when the only through road in Petersham, the A307, has been wholly or partly closed prove that the effects on Petersham especially are little short of catastrophic. All other areas bordering the Park have alternative routes of some kind, but Ham and Petersham, short of crossing two river bridges and taking a detour of six or seven miles, has none. Apart from this, the narrow A307 road is already unsuitable for the size and volume of traffic using it; extra traffic decanted from the Park roads cannot be accommodated easily, or reasonably.

Effective opposition to any proposal depends largely on time freely given by the committees of local Associations or of *ad hoc* groups formed to contest specific issues; all are short of willing hands in these tasks. The preservation and improvement of all that this book contains will be at risk unless caring residents are willing to devote their time to battles yet to come.

Richmond History
The following articles concerning Ham and Petersham have been printed in
this journal, published annually by the Richmond Local History Society, and
available for reference in the Local Studies Room of Richmond:
(1) 1981   Vincent van Gogh in Richmond and Petersham (Stephen
                Pasmore)
            Hesba Stretton, Novelist of Ivycroft, Ham Common (Silvia
                Greenwood)
            Richmond Schools in the 18th & 19th Centuries (Bernard J Bull)
(2) 1981   Richmond Miscellanies: From John Evelyn's *Diaries*
(3) 1982   Thomas Knyvett at Ham House in 1644
            St Andrew's Church, Ham (Silvia Greenwood)
(4) 1983   Old Petersham Lodge: A Royalist refuge (Stephen Pasmore)
            John Hoppner at Petersham
            A short history of Ham's development (Silvia Greenwood)
(5) 1984   Dinner at Pembroke Lodge, 1853
            Lord Camelford's visit to Petersham to challenge Capt. George
                Vancouver to a duel (Stephen Pasmore)
(6) 1985   Sir Everard Home on floods in Ham 1822
            Horace Walpole's visits to Richmond (Stephen Pasmore)
            A view near Richmond by Thomas Rowlandson (Stephen
                Pasmore)
            John Constable at Ham House (Stephen Pasmore)
(7) 1986   Lady Mary Coke and her Journal for 1766 (Stephen Pasmore)
            Who wrote the Richmond Park pamphlets? (Edward Casaubon)
            Petersham British School and the Russell family in Victorian
                times (George F Bartle)
            All Saints' Church, Petersham, in wartime (Gillian Hughes)
(8) 1989 James Boswell in Richmond Park (Stephen Pasmore)
(9) 1990 The early history of Ham Part I (John Cloake)
            The Countess of Pembroke & Pembroke Lodge (S. Pasmore)
            The milestones of Richmond-upon-Thames
(10) 1991 The Early History of Ham Part II (John Cloake)
            Four Lodges in Richmond Park (Diana Howard)
(11) 1992 New Park and an Indian doe (Stephen Pasmore)
            Charles Dickens sings the praises of Petersham in 1839
(12) 1993 Royalty in Petersham in 1769
            Sudbrook Lodge, Petersham Road (Stephen Pasmore)
            A brief history of Gordon, Forbes and Langham Houses on Ham
                Common (Evelyn Pritchard)

(13) 1994 Queen Charlotte visits Ham (Evelyn Pritchard)
      The site of the Cassel Hospital (Evelyn Pritchard)
      A white doe in Richmond Park (Stephen Pasmore)
      Charles Dickens at Petersham (Margaret Evans)
(14) 1995 Cardinal Newman and his boyhood in Ham (Stephen Pasmore)
      History of St Michael's Convent, Ham Common (Evelyn
          Pritchard)
(15) 1996 The fire at New Park, Petersham (Stephen Pasmore)
      Thatched House Lodge, Richmond Park, in 1918 (Stephen
          Pasmore)
      A Petersham Mystery (Richard J Smith)
      Myth and Reality on Richmond's Victorian Railways
          (Tim Sherwood)
(16) 1997 New light on old Petersham houses – I (John Cloake)
(17) 1998 New light on old Petersham houses – II (John Cloake)
      Hydropathy at Ham (Jackie Latham)
      Historic trees in Richmond, Petersham and Kew (Nigel Hepper)
(18) 1999 The two Lodges on Ham Common (Evelyn Pritchard)
      The Ham Street bend and the Great Barn of Ham (Evelyn
          Pritchard)
      Woodbine Cottage (John Beardmore)
(19) 2000 The Fight for the View from Richmond Hill (Ron Berryman)
      Robert Owen's 'Most Horrible and Demoralizing Discourse'
          (Jackie E M Latham)
      The Case of the Foolish Historians (Evelyn Pritchard)
      Ham Common and the Norths' Connection to Kew
          (Evelyn Pritchard)
      The 'Modernisation of Ham House' (John Moses)

General Bibliography

1. *Signposts to the past.* Place names in the history of England. Margaret Gelling. 1978.
2. *The Edwards Collection.* David Field. Richmond Local Studies Library Surrey Archaeological Collections 74, 1938, pp.169ff.
3. *The Making of the English Landscape.* W. G. Hoskins. Penguin Books.
4. *A History of Richmond Park.* C. L. Collenette. 1937.
5. *Richmond Park.* Pamela Fletcher Jones. Phillimore.
6. *The Building of St. Andrew's Church, Ham Common.* Evelyn Pritchard. Available from St. Andrew's Church.
7. *A walk around St. Andrew's Church.* Available from the Church.
8. *A portrait of Ham in Early Victorian times 1840–1860.* Evelyn Pritchard. 1991. Reprinted 1999 by Alma Publishers, Ham.
9. *The Complete Letters of Vincent van Gogh, Vol. I.* Thames & Hudson, 1958.
10. *History of St Peter's Church, Petersham, Surrey.* Charles D Warren. Sidgwick & Jackson, 1938. (Out of print.)
11. *Richmond, from Kew Green to Ham Common.* Kathleen Courlander. B T Batsford 1953.
12. *A Gossiping Guide to All Saints' Petersham.* W H Oxley, no date. (Out of print.)
13. *Richmond Herald, Christmas number,* 1908.
14. *The Village School.* June Lewis. Robert Hale, 1989.
15. *Life in Ham and Petersham 1933–1993 with the Ham and Petersham Association.* 1994
16. *Ham and Petersham Reminiscences.* M. L. Lansdale. Ham and Petersham Ratepayers' and Residents' Association. (Covers the years 1922–1956.)
17. *The Penny Post 1680–1918.* Frank Staff. 1964.
18. *Packhorse, wagon and coach.* J. Crofts. 1967.
19. *The Railways of Richmond upon Thames.* Tim Sherwood. Forge Books, 1991.
20. *The Thames Highway, Vol. II.* Fred S. Thacker.
21. *The Thames. Record of a working Waterway.* D. G. Wilson. 1987.
22. *London River.* Gavin Wightman.
23. *Twickenham Ferries in History and Song.* D. H Simpson and E. A. Morris. Twickenham Local History Society papers, 1980

24. *Ham and Petersham as it was*. James Green and Silvia Greenwood. Hendon Publishing Co. Ltd, 1980.
25. *Ham Manor Farm and Secrett's Farm.* Architectural notes and photograph of demolition, 1958. Surrey Record Office, Ref. CC32/21/12.
26. *Ham Lands. A Guide to Nature Conservation.* London Borough of Richmond upon Thames, undated.
27. *The Buildings of England. London2: South.* Bridget Cherry and Nikolaus Pevsner. Penguin Books 1983.
28. *Ham House and its owners through four centuries.* Evelyn Pritchard. Richmond Local History Society, 1998 reprint.
29. *G.B.S. on Music.* Penguin Books, 1962.
30. *Problems with Badgers.* RSPCA, Horsham.
31. *Richmond Park. The Walker's Historical Guide.* David McDowall, self-published, 1996.
32 *Richmond Park.* The Royal Parks. Crown Copyright 1993.

Index (*compiled by Anne Coles*)

Page numbers in italic refer to illustrations in text